20 full body programmes for exercise lovers

An essential guide to boosting your general fitness, strength, power and endurance

By

Darren O'Toole BSc

Discover more books and ebooks of interest to you and find out about the range of work we do at the forefront of health, fitness and wellbeing.

www.ymcaed.org.uk

Published by Central YMCA Trading Ltd (trading as YMCAed).
Registered Company No. 3667206.

Copyright © Central YMCA Trading Ltd 2013
All rights reserved. No part of this publication may be reproduced, stored in a retrieval system, or transmitted, in any form or by any means, without the prior permission of the publisher.

YMCAed
Central YMCA Trading Ltd
112 Great Russell Street
London
WC1B 3NQ

www.ymcaed.org.uk

ISBN: 1484072405
ISBN-13: 978-1484072400

This book is presented solely for educational and entertainment purposes. The author and publisher are not offering it as legal, medical, or other professional services advice. While best efforts have been used in preparing this book, the author and publisher make no representations or warranties of any kind and assume no liabilities of any kind with respect to the accuracy or completeness of the contents and specifically disclaim any implied warranties of merchantability or fitness of use for a particular purpose. Neither the publisher nor the individual author(s) shall be liable for any physical, psychological, emotional, financial, or commercial damages, including, but not limited to, special, incidental, consequential or other damages, resulting from the information or programs contained herein. Every person is different and the information, advice and programs contained herein may not be suitable for your situation. Exercise is not without its risks and, as such, we would strongly advise that you consult with your healthcare professional before beginning any programme of exercise, especially if you have, or suspect you may have, any injuries or illnesses, are currently pregnant or have recently given birth. The advice, information and guidance given in Central YMCA Guides is in no way intended as a substitute for medical consultation. As with any form of exercise, you should stop immediately if you feel faint, dizzy or have physical discomfort or pain or any other contra indication, and consult a physician.

Central YMCA is the world's founding YMCA. Established in 1844 in Central London, it was the first YMCA to open its doors and, in so doing, launched a movement that has now grown to become the world's biggest youth organisation. Today, Central YMCA is the UK's leading health, fitness and wellbeing charity, committed to helping people from all walks of life – and specifically the young and those with a specific need – to live happier, healthier and more fulfilled lives.

CONTENTS

	About the author	7
	Introduction	9
1	Set your goals	11
2	No time for excuses	17
3	How hard are you working?	21
4	General fitness - *Programme 1* - *Programme 2* - *Programme 3* - *Programme 4*	23
5	Endurance - *Programme 5* - *Programme 6* - *Programme 7* - *Programme 8* - *Programme 9*	35
6	Strength - *Programme 10* - *Programme 11* - *Programme 12* - *Programme 13* - *Programme 14* - *Programme 15*	49
7	Power - *Programme 16* - *Programme 17* - *Programme 18*	67
8	Ultimate conditioning workouts - *Programme 19* - *Programme 20*	77
	References	81
	Also out now	83

ABOUT THE AUTHOR

Thank you for reading my book.

I'm a sport scientist and fully qualified personal trainer. Having gained a BSc (Hons) in Sport Science, I worked at Watford and West Ham United football clubs in strength and conditioning roles. Working in elite sport showed me just what dedication and effort is required to reach the very top of any sport, and the significance of a well-structured, periodised training plan in getting there. I have used these principles ever since and hopefully this book will give you an insight into their importance.

On a personal note, I've been a fitness fanatic for as long as I can remember. It began with an immense passion for sport – from football to tennis via cross country running and cricket – and has since seen me trying my hand at every new and intriguing training approach I come across. Indeed, if it's good enough for the professionals, then it's good enough for the rest of us too.

This book is a culmination of years of training, reading, studying and embracing all things fitness. I hope it will help to ignite a similar passion in you and push you on to achieve your personal best.

Good luck.

Darren

Central YMCA Health and Fitness Guides

INTRODUCTION

The benefits of exercise and training are well-documented and largely well-known to us all. Whether it is for physical and mental health, or for sporting performance, most of us know that we should be taking part in some form of physical activity.

Yet the reality is that many people simply don't do enough, which is puzzling. Indeed, it is rare in today's 24/7 society to find something that can elicit so many rewards. Go to the cinema and, if you're lucky, you get two hours of enjoyment. Eat out and you'll cherish the meal, the drink and the dessert, but this will only last until the end of the evening at best, or until the bill arrives.

However, a good training session can offer benefits which last for days, and beyond. Indeed, an effective and well-structured training programme should ensure that you achieve many of your long-term goals, from looking good and feeling stronger, to developing power and running faster. This, in turn, will do wonders for your confidence and self-esteem, while also providing you with significant health benefits that will offer you far greater payback than your outlandish meal out or the memory of your evening at the cinema.

It's perhaps fair to assume that, by purchasing this book, you have at least a basic grasp of the general benefits of training and the need to do something on a regular basis. This puts us at the perfect starting point to set and achieve some fitness goals, and over the coming pages we'll cover the best methods to do so.

Of course, for those of us interested in fitness there are plenty of options out there to help us achieve our goals. You can be sure a new craze – whether it is a new dance class, piece of equipment or training approach – is just around the corner, ready to entice you with promises of rapid results.

I believe that all these new ideas have a place in this exciting industry, just as long as there are clear benefits to them and they don't have a negative effect on your ultimate training goal, or make too much of a dent in your wallet. So, whilst the training programmes that I have devised in this book do not endorse any of these new fads, and I do stick closely to the more tried and tested approaches, I'd encourage readers to give everything a go, at least once and budget permitting. Get out of your comfort zone, see what it offers and make your educated decision.

If you feel that your fitness goals can be achieved solely from attending three aerobics classes per week, then fantastic; all I ask is that you look at the principles that I put forward here and if you still arrive at the same conclusion then you're doing so in a way that is likely to garner results.

The golden rule, train hard, but above all else, enjoy yourself.

HOW TO USE THIS BOOK

I've separated the training programmes you'll encounter in this book into four overriding fitness or health goals, namely, general fitness, strength, endurance and power.

Each training programme has been drawn up to cover three fitness levels – low, medium and high – meaning that there is a programme here for everybody. If you know the areas that you want to improve, then feel free to go straight to that chapter. However, I'd recommend that you stop off at the chapter on goal setting (Chapter 1) to guarantee that you are laying the foundations for success.

I've designed these ready-made programmes to make your training a little easier. You can arrive for your session with the simple task of performing what is written on the page and, when this is no longer challenging enough, you can simply move on to the next level. It's as straightforward as that.

1

SET YOUR GOALS

WHAT ARE GOALS?

To gain the most out of this book, goal setting will play a pivotal role. However, to establish your own goals we must first ask ourselves what we mean by the term 'goal'.

Essentially those of us who train in gyms, studios, at home or outdoors will all have some element of motivation for undertaking the activity for which we have just put on our trainers and shorts to do. Experience has shown me, however, that, when asked, people will all too frequently deny having any goals at all. A gentle probe will soon reveal this to be untrue as a simple, 'I want to stay fit', or 'I want to be less tired', is as much of a goal as 'I want to run a marathon', or 'I want to lose 10 stone'.

It is important to take a few moments to drill down into these objectives, however simple, in order to develop a training programme which will work for you. Yes, this will take time and effort, but what is the point in training at all if you don't do so in a way that will ultimately bring about the results that you want? Therefore, the work you do at home with pen and paper to define your goals should be seen as the foundations for your training regimen.

Put simply, goal setting improves performance by directing attention, increasing effort and persistence and is a positive motivational tool. For goal setting to work, however, it must be well-planned. An effective goal should be written down and monitored regularly to ascertain whether any progress is being made. For some reason, people can decide upon their goals and then ignore them only to return after a number of months to see if they were successful. Instead, and for a greater chance of success, let's define our goals and then check our progress on a weekly basis. Far from being an arduous task, we can use our goals and progress checks as a tool to motivate us for the following week's training.

For goals to be effective, try aligning them to the SMART acronym (Specific, Measurable, Achievable, Realistic and Time-framed). These apply to settings outside of fitness too, so they may already be familiar to you.

As we discuss developing your SMART goals, why not make notes on aspects of your own goals as we go...

Specific Goals

This refers to a goal that focuses exactly on what needs to be achieved. For instance, 'I want to get fit' would not be considered a specific goal. However, 'I want to beat my personal best for a 10k run', or even, 'I want to be able to run 10k' would be. By defining a goal in this manner, it will make you accountable to the results. If your goals aren't specific it can be too easy to accept your level of attainment, so make them clearly defined to ensure that it becomes a challenge for you.

Measurable Goals

As with a goal being specific, if it cannot be measured then there is no way of establishing if you have succeeded. By quantifying your goal, you'll understand how near you are to achieving it.

Achievable Goals

Essentially once you've set your goals, you have set out on a journey whereby you are committing a period of time, effort and energy into achieving them. It is therefore extremely important to ensure that you can actually achieve them from the outset. For a non-runner to declare, 'I want to run a sub three hour marathon in four weeks' is simply not going to happen. So make sure that your goals can be achieved.

REALISTIC GOALS

Although similar to achievable, this aspect of goal setting takes into account your lifestyle, commitments and resources. If you are planning on running a marathon, but you know that over the next three month period you have two weddings, a business trip and a holiday planned, then are you being realistic about your goal? If you set goals which you soon realise are not realistic and achievable, you are likely to abort the training programme very early on. When creating your goals, plot all of the major events and commitments that you have over that period on a calendar. Then judge whether you believe it is realistic and, if not, adjust your goals from the outset.

TIME-FRAMED GOALS

Throughout your training programme, you will inevitably encounter days when your motivation is a little low. However, by outlining the time-frame in which you want to achieve your goals, your determination will hopefully offset this. It serves no real purpose to define a goal and undertake a programme without deciding when you want your goal to be achieved. So, again, make sure that the time you give yourself is realistic.

Now, having established that your goals are SMART, I'd like you to write them down. However, before you do so, I'll offer you one further consideration. Much of the research into goal setting has looked at the difficulty of the goal in relation to achieving a successful outcome. So, with this in mind, I believe that the best goals are those that present you with a moderate level of difficulty, i.e. not too difficult and not easy.

It seems obvious really. Goals which are too easy will offer no real sense of achievement as they can be attained with a minimal level of commitment or effort, whilst goals that are very difficult will seem so daunting that you will be put off by the likelihood of failure and therefore give up before you've even really got going.

With all of these areas considered, look at your SMART goal and decide whether you think that it fits into the 'moderate' difficulty range, i.e. that which is most suited to success.

Now that you've set your overarching long-term goal, it makes sense to come up with some short-term goals to help you along the way. Indeed, without short-term goals, you may blindly believe that you are on track only to ultimately discover that you are a little short of your target. The last thing you want to discover at the end of your programme is that if you'd stepped up your intensity or commitment just a couple of weeks before, you would have been successful.

In other words, by cutting your overarching long-term goal into bite size chunks, you'll be able to monitor if you are on course for success and amend your plans accordingly.

How you set these short-term goals is completely up to you – weekly, fortnightly, monthly – but I'd recommend that you aim for a minimum of four short-term targets within your plan to give yourself the best possibility of success; remembering to make each short-term target SMART.

To help you along the way, here are a few examples of goals and how they can be broken down into shorter-term targets.

Goal setting: Example 1

Long-term goal: To drop two dress sizes in time to attend a wedding in the summer
Short-term goals:
End of week two – Eat breakfast and five pieces of fruit and vegetable every day
End of the first month – Take part in one cardio, one resistance and one mixed session for each of the first four weeks
End of the second month – Run for 5km continuously for the first time, also to have dropped one dress size
End of the third month – No alcoholic drinks consumed for the whole month

If this example is similar to your goals, make sure you read Chapter 4 on training for general fitness.

Goal setting - Example 2

Long-term goal: To run a marathon in six months, completing it in less than three and a half hours
Short-term goals:
End of the first month – To run for one hour continuously
End of the second month – To run for one hour incorporating 5x4 minute intervals of faster than race pace speed (12.1km/h)

End of the third month – To run for two hours continuously
End of the fourth month – To complete a half marathon race in one hour 45 minutes
End of the fifth month – To have run a distance of 23 miles

If this example is similar to your goals, make sure you read Chapter 5 on endurance training.

Goal setting - Example 3

Long-term goal: To increase one-rep-max on the squat by 10kg in one month
Short-term goals:
End of session 2 – To have gained three-rep-max and five-rep-max scores for the squat
End of session 4 – Perform 3 sets of 3 reps at 90% one-rep-max
End of session 6 – Perform 3 sets of 3 reps at 95% one-rep-max
End of session 8 – Perform 3 reps at the previous one-rep-max weight

If this example is similar to your goals, make sure you read Chapter 6 on strength training.

Goal setting - Example 4

Long-term goal: To increase long jump personal best to 6.80 metres (10cm increase) in time for the county championships in 10 weeks
Short-term goals:
End of week 2 – Film, analyse and develop efficiency of jumping performance
End of week 4 – 30m sprint personal best
End of week 6 – Standing long jump improvement by at least 3cm
End of week 8 – New 30m sprint personal best

If this example is similar to your goals, make sure you read Chapter 7 on power training.

2

NO TIME FOR EXCUSES

There are a whole host of reasons why people decide not to exercise and it would be foolish to put this book together without addressing this topic. The aim of this book is to make your training structured and easy to follow, as well as hopefully guiding you towards the results you're after. However, all this will require commitment and dedication on your part. So here are a few potential barriers to exercise and some tips for overcoming them.

1. INTERNAL BARRIERS TO EXERCISE

Just as the name suggests, internal barriers refer to those thoughts, feelings and perceptions inside us all that relate to exercise. These are often personal to the individual and can include such concerns as:

FEELINGS OF INTIMIDATION AND EMBARRASSMENT

Entering a fitness facility and starting to use weights and/or equipment that is unfamiliar to you can feel intimidating, particularly in an environment where everyone else appears super confident. However, it's worth remembering that exercising is a very personal and individual thing. When people are in the gym, they are invariably focused on themselves and often the only ones who pay attention to others are either the instructors or those who are also feeling insecure. Also, remember that most of the people around you have more than likely had the same levels of apprehension in the past, so they all know what you may be experiencing. Be patient and you'll ultimately feel at ease in the fitness environment.

LOW SELF-ESTEEM AND SELF-CONFIDENCE

If you don't feel confident about yourself or your ability to exercise on a regular basis, then this can dent your own belief in your ability to achieve your goals, which ultimately impacts on your motivation. If this is a concern then pay greater attention to your goal setting. Setting yourself realistic short-term goals will enable you to achieve your long-term goals in bite size chunks. This will slowly build your confidence a help you to progress through your training programme.

PERCEIVED LACK OF TIME

Do regular exercisers have any more time than non-exercisers? Of course not, it is merely a question of how we choose to use our time each day. Replace sitting on the sofa, watching TV or visits to your local coffee shop with exercise and you're likely to discover more than enough time to fit in some training.

If you actually plot the hours you are in work, together with your out-of-work commitments, then you'll soon note that there are often empty spaces in the day that can offer you more than enough time for exercise. Block out three or four of these gaps per week and make this your exercise commitment. If you've got young children and can't get out in the evenings, then why not use your journeys to work and your lunchtimes to fit in your training time?

Talking of time, you'll be pleased to know that the training programmes in this book don't require you to commit to a huge amount of time each week.

PERCEIVED INCONVENIENCE

Inconvenience can be perceived even when it's not a reality, leading many to believe that exercise is too much bother. Changing a daily routine involves a significant change in behaviour and requires effort. Just remember that the benefits to your health and mood will far outweigh the small period of time where you feel that this additional commitment is an inconvenience.

2. EXTERNAL BARRIERS TO EXERCISE

If you have been strong and committed and fought all of the internal barriers which may prevent you from taking part in your exercise routine, then the last thing you want is for external factors to add to your motivational challenges. However, societal changes that have reduced the time available for exercise and environmental changes that may discourage people from exercising can both be major obstacles when committing to a training programme. Thankfully, there are solutions to these external barriers.

TECHNOLOGY

Advances in technology have contributed to a physically inactive population. The developments in computers and communication technology have reduced people's activity levels. Television, computer games, mobile phones, social networking and the internet take up a large proportion of our leisure time. However, technology can also be used as a positive.

Use your iPod to put together a motivational playlist which will inspire you to workout. Put on some of your favourite tracks and only allow yourself a listen when you're working out.

Also, evaluate the stresses caused by your phones, emails and social media accounts. Whilst technology has brought some positive benefits to our lives, it also means that we are now contactable at all times. Again, use your workout as 'contact-free time' and start to de-stress by forgetting about the pressures of everyday life.

WORK

Work brings with it a degree of stress and inevitably requires a time commitment on your part. However, there's no reason why you can't fit exercise around your working life. As I mentioned previously, the commute to work – which for many can be as much as 1-2 hours per day – could be replaced with a cycle or a run. Even if your hours at work are long, you're still likely to have two days off per week. The programmes won't take you too long to complete either, guaranteeing that you can fit two sessions in on your days off. All you then need to do is find time for one additional session during the week, so why not use your commute or lunchtimes to fit this in?

FAMILY

Weekdays for many families are filled with work-related obligations, while weekends fill up quickly with family time, chores and errands. However, it is possible to fit exercise around the supermarket shop or the swimming gala. Indeed, if you're taking your children to a swimming gala, then why not take a dip for yourself, or if they're playing football, use the space around the pitches for a workout of your own.

If you're stuck indoors looking after the little ones, you could always make the most of those magic moments when they're asleep or preoccupied and jump on a reasonably priced exercise bike, or piece together a workout around your home.

Of course, if you're child-free but duty bound to spend the weekends with your significant other, then get them involved too and get the best of both worlds. Go out for a run or to the gym together and then reward yourselves with a coffee or a meal out. You'll spend the whole day together and have enjoyed a shared challenge.

Hopefully now, whatever your barriers to exercise, you can see that there is usually a simple way to overcome these obstacles and pursue your training programme. Remember, if you are unsure of whether the solution will work for you, then simply give it a trial period. Be patient and be committed and the benefits will far outweigh any extra effort.

3

HOW HARD ARE YOU WORKING?

Today the majority of gym equipment comes with a built-in heart rate monitor which will offer you a quick reference guide to your exertion levels while you're exercising. Other heart-rate gadgets can be purchased for a relatively low cost to monitor your levels when you are exercising outside or weight training. Another very useful way of monitoring the intensity of your exercise is through a rate of perceived exertion (RPE) scale.

THE RPE SCALE

The RPE scale (Borg and Linderholm, 1967) was formulated to enable individuals to see clearly how hard they are working. The scale runs from 6 to 20 reflecting heart rates ranging from 60 to 200 beats per minute with descriptions to suggest the intensity of the activity.

Thankfully, an adapted scale – the Borg CR-10 scale – has been developed to be a little easier to use. The CR-10 is a category scale with numbers relating to verbal expressions, which allows comparison between intensities as well as a determination of intensity levels.

For the purposes of this book, we'll use the Borg CR-10 scale to quantify exertion levels within the training programmes. This will give you a quick snapshot of whether you are working at the intensity you should be. To make this work most effectively, I'd recommend that you have the scale with you, that you decide how hard you've been working and then check against where you should be. This way, you'll easily see whether you are working too hard, or not hard enough.

BORG'S CR-10 SCALE

0	Nothing at all
1	Extremely light – just noticeable that activity is taking place
2	Light – very gentle aspect of a warm up
3	Moderate – an easy to maintain intensity
4	Somewhat hard – a noticeable change in breathing pattern but still a comfortable level to maintain this intensity
5	Hard – a challenging intensity which can be maintained but with some element of discomfort
6	(Borg left some numbers blank)
7	Very hard – breathing is very heavy and this intensity is tough to maintain but possible
8	(Borg left some numbers blank)
9	Almost maximal – You can continue this intensity for a very limited period of time
10	Maximal effort – no extra effort is possible and you can only maintain this output for a very short period before your body gives up

Adapted from: Borg GAV. *Borg's Rating of Perceived Exertion and Pain Scales*. Champaign, IL: Human Kinetics, 1998.

4

GENERAL FITNESS

In my experience as a personal trainer the vast majority of clients come to me for improvements in their general health and wellbeing. They may not articulate it in such explicit terms, but their varied goals are all aimed at a healthier and happier lifestyle. Whether this is simply being able to perform everyday activities without getting out of breath, losing weight, or being fit enough to return to playing sport, these all look to improve both physical and mental health.

BENEFITS OF PHYSICAL ACTIVITY

Some of the benefits of taking part in regular physical activity aimed at improving general fitness levels include:

WEIGHT CONTROL/FAT LOSS

If exercise is new to you then, in the simplest terms, it will see you burning more calories than you had previously been doing. So if you were putting on weight then you are likely, first of all, to go into a maintenance stage. However, if you were maintaining your weight then you are going to create a calorie deficit which will result in fat/weight loss.

STRONGER BONES AND MUSCLES

Regular exercise can lower the risk of muscular injuries from day-to-day activities by ensuring stronger muscles, better posture and improved technique. You'll also be less likely to suffer from age-related problems such as osteoporosis in later life.

FEELING BETTER ABOUT LIFE

Exercise triggers the production of endorphins. It is believed that these are produced as natural pain relievers in response to the shock that the body receives during exercise. Though it's not just endorphins that have an effect on your emotions; exercise also increases levels of serotonin, dopamine and norepinephrine. These neurotransmitters have been associated with elevated mood, and work in the same way as antidepressant medications.

REDUCE YOUR RISK OF CARDIOVASCULAR DISEASE

Regular physical activity lowers the prevalence of cardiovascular disease, reduces blood pressure and improves cholesterol levels. In addition, sedentary behaviour is independently associated with type 2 diabetes, some types of cancer and metabolic dysfunction. The chances of such impactful ailments and the subsequent increase in life expectancy are a fantastic motivation for those starting an exercise regimen.

ARE YOU DOING ENOUGH?

In the UK, The Chief Medical Officer's published guidance for physical activity levels (http://www.dh.gov.uk/prod_consum_dh/groups/dh_digitalassets/documents/digitalasset/dh_128210.pdf / *ymcaed.org.uk/pal*) for adults aged between 19 and 64 years old is one reliable measure for assessing whether you're currently doing enough exercise.

According to the CMO's 2011 report, Start Active, Stay Active (see link above), adults should aim to be active on a daily basis. Over a week, activity should add up to at least 150 minutes of moderate intensity activity in bouts of 10 minutes or more – the equivalent of 30 minutes of exercise, five times per week.

Alternatively, comparable benefits can be achieved through 75 minutes of vigorous activity spread across the week, or a combination of moderate or vigorous activity.

Adults should undertake physical activity to improve muscle strength on at least two days a week.

All adults should also minimise the amount of time spent being sedentary (sitting) for extended periods.

These guidelines form the basis for the training programmes that have been devised in this chapter. Of course the guidelines relating to level of intensity leave you with a decision to make. Would you prefer to undertake moderate activity, vigorous training or a mix of the two? I've summarised the differences in these terms to help you to make your decision.

MODERATE INTENSITY ACTIVITY

This refers to an intensity that causes you to work within a heart rate zone of 55-70% of maximum heart rate. This is a region which is fairly comfortable for the exerciser, but does indicate a small element of exertion. This intensity may work well for someone who has been inactive for a considerable period of time and has only just begun a programme of physical activity.

As a rule, maximum heart rate can be worked out by this very simple equation (Fox et al., 1971):

Maximum heart rate = 220 − your age

The relationship between the amount of exercise performed and the extent of the health benefits reaped from that programme is termed the 'dose-response relationship'. The relationship shows that higher levels of intensity and duration of exercise are associated with improved health benefits, although this does level off, and the rationale for further increasing the workload would no longer be to improve health, but instead to improve endurance performance.

With this in mind it would seem obvious to think that we all need to train for longer and at a greater intensity. Up to a point this is true. Yet it must be acknowledged that people who are new to exercise were previously not doing it for a reason and by solely offering long or high intensity sessions we would be ignoring those exercisers who need a structured programme to achieve their goals. This is the main reason for offering the alternative training approaches in this book.

VIGOROUS ACTIVITY

One alternative for obtaining the recommended level of physical activity is to work at a higher level of intensity. Vigorous activity refers to an intensity that causes you to work within 70-80% of your maximum heart rate. Whilst the obvious benefit is that of the limited time you will need to exercise, the downside is that it is more challenging and as such will feel more unpleasant to do.

THE IMPORTANCE OF A THOROUGH WARM UP

To reduce your risk of injury and to mentally prepare you for the workout to follow, completing a thorough warm up is absolutely essential. The warm up should consist of three key sections – a pulse raiser, mobility exercises and some preparatory stretches. The pulse raiser involves completing four to five minutes of exercise to raise your heart rate and increase the blood flow to your working muscles. Choose the exercise wisely based upon the session to follow, e.g. if you are to complete a lower body workout then cycling would be a very appropriate choice of pulse raiser. This should be completed at an intensity to elicit an RPE rating of 4.

You should then spend a short period of time mobilising the spine through a mix of side bends and trunk rotations – focusing on your hips facing forwards throughout. You can then choose whether you want to undertake dynamic or static stretches. Dynamic stretches are slow, controlled movements through the full range of motion whilst static stretches involve holding the stretch in a single position for 10-15 seconds. I advocate the use of dynamic stretches as they prepare the muscles in a more specific manner for the session to follow; you rarely find yourself holding a position in any exercise for as long as you would in a static stretch. But as part of the purpose of a warm up is to psychologically prepare for the session, choose the format of stretches that ensure you feel most ready for your workout.

YOUR GENERAL FITNESS TRAINING PROGRAMMES

Please make sure that you complete a thorough warm up (as described above) before taking part in any of the sessions in this book.

Key to the programme jargon
The training programmes include a few figures and references that may seem a bit puzzling at first glance, but hopefully this key will clarify things for you:

- *15 (3)* = 15 repetitions (3 sets)
- *20mins (2)* = 20 minutes (2 sets)
- *10mins (RPE 4)* = 10 minutes to be completed at an intensity of 4 on the rate of perceived exertion scale
- *75s:45s (RPE 5:9)* = 75 seconds to be completed at an intensity of 5:9 on the rate of perceived exertion scale immediately followed by 45 seconds at level 9
- *5 (3) (85%)* = 5 repetitions (3 sets) (Using a weight which is 85% of your five-rep-max)
- *10 (2) (65%)* = 10 repetitions (2 sets) (Using a weight which is 65% of your 10-rep-max)
- *15 (3) Medium* = 15 repetitions (3 sets) to be completed at a medium intensity
- *Super sets* = Completing two exercises immediately after each other with no rest between exercises. Rest should be taken before completing the next super set
- *Tri sets* = Completing three exercises, all of which challenge the same muscle group, immediately after each other with no rest between exercises. Rest should be taken before completing the next tri set
- *Giant sets* = Completing four exercises, all of which challenge the same muscle group, immediately after each other with no rest between exercises. Rest should be taken before completing the next giant set
- *Strip sets* = Completing as many repetitions as possible with a weight that you should ideally be only able to lift for 6-8 repetitions. Once you can lift no more (failure), you immediately choose a lower weight and continue the exercise until you reach failure once more. You must reach failure at four different weights before you rest
- *Ascending pyramids* = Completing multiple sets of the same exercise to challenge muscular endurance, size and strength by alternating the weight and repetitions in an ascending pyramid format
- *Full pyramids* = Completing multiple sets of the same exercise to challenge muscular endurance, size and strength by alternating the weight and repetitions in a full pyramid format
- *MB* = Medicine ball
- *DB* = Dumbbell
- *Interval* = alternating intensities within the same exercise
- *Pre-exhaust* = involves tiring a certain muscle using an isolation or 'single-

> joint' exercise before following it up with a compound or 'multiple-joint' exercise. This approach ensures that your larger muscles fatigue in the compound exercise at the same rate as the synergist (supporting) muscles. Often in exercises such as bench press, it may be your shoulders or triceps (synergists) that fatigue before your chest – limiting the training benefits. A pre-exhaust approach ensures this is not the case.
> ☐ Post-exhaust = involves completing a compound exercise followed by isolating the targeted muscle. This approach gives your training a real boost by demanding your muscles to perform in an isolated way when they are already fatigued.
>
> *Continuous* = maintaining one intensity throughout an exercise

PROGRAMME 1:

Type of programme: General fitness
Level: Entry programme (perfect for those new to exercise)

Week 1

SESSION ONE: Walk 10mins (2) (RPE 4)
SESSION TWO: Ab crunches; Plank; Bridge; Press ups; Superman; Triceps dips; Step ups; Squats 30secs (4)
SESSION THREE: Walk 15mins (2) (RPE 4)
SESSION FOUR: Dyna-band exercises: Low row; Upright row; Biceps curls; Shoulder press; Front raise 15 (3); Side steps; Heel flicks; High knees; Narrow lunges 30secs (3)

Week 2

SESSION ONE: Walk 15mins (2) (RPE 4)
SESSION TWO: Walk 20mins (2) (RPE 5)
SESSION THREE: Cycle 10mins (RPE 5); **X-Trainer** 10mins (RPE 5)
SESSION FOUR: Walk 20mins (2) (RPE 5)

Week 3

SESSION ONE: Run 5mins (3) (RPE 4)
SESSION TWO: Ab crunches; Plank; Bridge; Press ups; Superman; Triceps dips; Step ups; Squats 40secs (4)
SESSION THREE: Cycle 10mins (RPE 4); **Row** 4mins (2) (RPE 5); **X-Trainer** 6mins (2) (RPE 6)
SESSION FOUR: Dyna-band exercises: Low row; Upright row; Biceps curls; Shoulder press; Front raise 15 (3); Side steps; Heel flicks; High knees;

Narrow lunges 45secs (3)

Week 4

SESSION ONE: Cycle 10mins (RPE 4); **Row** 4mins (2) (RPE 5); **X-Trainer** 6mins (2) (RPE 5)
SESSION TWO: Run 5mins (4) (RPE 4)
SESSION THREE: Ab crunches; Plank; Bridge; Press ups; Superman; Triceps dips; Step ups; Squats 1min (3)
SESSION FOUR: Run 5mins (4) (RPE 4)

Week 5

SESSION ONE: Run 10mins (3) (RPE 5)
SESSION TWO: Squats; Calf raises; Lunges; Step ups; High knee jog; Side lunges; Bridge 1min (3)
SESSION THREE: Run 10mins (3) (RPE 5)
SESSION FOUR: Dyna-band exercises: Low row; Upright row; Biceps curls; Shoulder press; Front raise 20 (3); Side steps; Heel flicks; High knees; Narrow lunges 60secs (3)

Week 6

SESSION ONE: Cycle 12mins (RPE 5); **X-Trainer** 12mins (RPE 5)
SESSION TWO: Run 15mins (2) (RPE 5)
SESSION THREE: Squats; Calf raises; Lunges; Step ups; High knee jog; Side lunges; Bridge 1min (4)
SESSION FOUR: Run 15mins (2) (RPE 5)

Week 7

SESSION ONE: Super sets: DB Shoulder press; Lat raise; Chest flyes; Press ups; Lat pulldown; Single arm row; Biceps curl; Triceps pushdowns; Ab crunches; Russian twists 20(2) (RPE 5)
SESSION TWO: Run 15mins (2) (RPE 5)
SESSION THREE: X-Trainer 20mins (RPE 5)
SESSION FOUR: Run 20mins; 10mins (RPE 5)

Week 8

SESSION ONE: Super sets: DB Shoulder press; Lat raise; Chest flyes; Press ups; Lat pulldown; Single arm row; Biceps curl; Triceps pushdowns;

Ab crunches; Russian twists 15(3) (RPE 5)
SESSION TWO: Run 20mins; 15mins (RPE 5)
SESSION THREE: Squats; Calf raises; Lunges; Step ups; High knee jog; Side lunges; Bridge 1min (5)
SESSION FOUR: Run 30mins (RPE 5)

PROGRAMME 2:
Type of programme: General fitness
Level: Medium fitness programme (perfect for those who have exercised intermittently over the last year)

Week 1

SESSION ONE: Run 15mins (2) (RPE 5)
SESSION TWO: Row 1km (RPE 5); **Cycle** 15mins (RPE 6)
SESSION THREE: Squats; Calf raises; Lunges; Step ups; High knee jog; Side lunges; Bridge 50secs (3)

Week 2

SESSION ONE: Cycle 10mins (RPE 4); **Row** 4mins (2) (RPE 5); **X-Trainer** 6mins (2) (RPE 5)
SESSION TWO: Ab crunches; Plank; Bridge; Press ups; Superman; Triceps dips; Step ups; Squats 1min (3)
SESSION THREE: Run 20mins (2) (RPE 6)

Week 3

SESSION ONE: Cycle 12mins (RPE 5); **X-Trainer** 12mins (RPE 5)
SESSION TWO: Run 15mins (RPE 5); 10mins (RPE 6); 5mins (RPE 7)
Rest 2mins between sets
SESSION THREE: Squats; Calf raises; Lunges; Step ups; High knee jog; Side lunges; Bridge 45secs (4)

Week 4

SESSION ONE: Run 25mins (2) (RPE 6)
SESSION TWO: Ab crunches; Plank; Superman; Side plank; Leg drops; Bridge 1min (4)
SESSION THREE: Squats 15(3) (65%); Deadlift 15(3) (65%); Bench

press 15(3) (65%); Bent over row 15(3) (65%); Shoulder press 15(3) (65%)

Week 5

SESSION ONE: Post exhaust: Bench press; Triceps dips; Lat pulldown; Narrow grip pulldown; Squats;
Leg extension; Shoulder press; Prone lat raise 12 (3) (65%)
SESSION TWO: Rotator cuffs: External rotation; Internal rotation; Horizontal abduction; Horizontal adduction; Prone raise; Lat raise; Superman; Bridge; Plank 1min (3)
SESSION THREE: Burpees; Squat jumps; Squat thrusts; Mountain climbers; Lunges 10(4)

Week 6

SESSION ONE: Super sets: DB Shoulder press; Lat raise; Chest flyes; Press ups; Lat pulldown; Single arm row; Biceps curl; Triceps pushdowns; Ab crunches; Russian twists 15(3) (RPE 6)
SESSION TWO: Leg extension; Leg curl; Lunges; Leg press; Calf raises 12 (4); Run 15mins (RPE 6)
SESSION THREE: Row Continuous 5mins (RPE 5); Interval (RPE 10:4)10s:50s; 20s:40s; 30s:30s; 20s:40s; 10s:50s (Rest 1min) (2)

Week 7

SESSION ONE: Run 30mins (RPE 6)
SESSION TWO: Ascending pyramids: Chest press; Lat pulldown; Shoulder press; Squats; Biceps curl; Triceps pushdown; Intensity: 15 (55%); 12 (60%); 10 (65%); 8 (70%); 5(80%).
SESSION THREE: Cycle 15mins (RPE 6); **X-Trainer** 20mins (RPE 5)

Week 8

SESSION ONE: Row 1500m; **Cycle** 10km; **Run** 2km
SESSION TWO: Run 40mins (RPE 6)
SESSION THREE: Squats; Calf raises; Lunges; Step ups; High knee jog; Side lunges; Bridge; Plank 1min (5)

PROGRAMME 3:
Type of programme: General fitness
Level: High fitness programme (perfect for those who have completed the medium fitness programme previously or anyone who has regularly trained over the last year)

Week 1

SESSION ONE: Run 25mins (RPE 6)
SESSION TWO: Ab crunches; Plank; Superman; Side plank; Leg drops; Bridge 1min(5)
SESSION THREE: Squats 15(3) (65%); Deadlift 15(3) (65%); Bench press 15(3) (65%); Bent over row 15(3) (65%); Shoulder press 15(3) (65%)

Week 2

SESSION ONE: Post exhaust: Bench press; Triceps dips; Lat pulldown; Narrow grip pulldown;
Squats; Leg extension; Shoulder press; Prone lat raise 12(3) (70%)
SESSION TWO: Row Continuous 5mins (RPE 5); Interval 100m:150m (RPE 9:6)(4); **Cycle** 15mins (RPE 7)
SESSION THREE: Burpees; Squat jumps; Squat thrusts; Mountain climbers; Lunges 20(3)

Week 3

SESSION ONE: Super sets: DB Shoulder press; Lat raise; Chest flyes; Press ups; Lat pulldown; Single arm row; Biceps curl; Triceps pushdowns 10 (4) (70%)
SESSION TWO: Leg extension; Leg curl; Lunges; Leg press; Calf raises 10(4) (80%); Run 15mins (RPE 7)
SESSION THREE: Row Continuous 5mins (RPE 5); Interval (RPE 10:4) 10s:50s; 20s:40s; 30s:30s; 40s:20s; 50s:10s (Rest 1min) (2)

Week 4

SESSION ONE: Run 30mins (RPE 7)
SESSION TWO: Ab crunches; Plank; Superman; Side plank; Leg drops; Bridge; Weighted crunches 1min(5)
SESSION THREE: Cycle 15mins (RPE 7); **X-Trainer** 20mins (RPE 7)

Week 5

SESSION ONE: Row 1500m; **Cycle** 10km; **Run** 2km (timed)
SESSION TWO: Run 40mins (RPE 7)
SESSION THREE: Ascending pyramids: Chest press; Lat pulldown; Shoulder press; Squats; Biceps curl; Triceps pushdown; Intensity: 15 (60%); 12 (70%); 10 (75%); 8 (80%); 5(90%).

Week 6

SESSION ONE: Giant sets: DB Shoulder press; Lat raise; Upright row; Prone raise; Chest flyes; Press ups; Decline press; Incline press; Lat pulldown; Single arm row; Pull ups; Bent arm pullover 10(4) (75%)
SESSION TWO: Run 45mins (RPE 6)
SESSION THREE: Row 1500m; **Cycle** 10km; **Run** 2km (timed to beat week 6)

Week 7

SESSION ONE: Squats 10(4) (80%); Deadlift 10(4) (80%); Bench press 10(4) (80%); Bent over row 10(4) (80%); Shoulder press 10(4) (80%)
SESSION TWO: Run 30mins (RPE 6); 20mins (RPE 7); 10mins (RPE 8)
(Rest 3mins between sets)
SESSION THREE: Press ups; Burpees; Squat jumps; Dumbbell punches (2x2-4kg); Mountain climbers; Lunges 15(4); **Row** 1km (RPE 7)

Week 8

SESSION ONE: Row 2km; **Cycle** 12km; **Run** 3km
SESSION TWO: Squats 10(4) (85%); Deadlift 10(4) (85%); Bench press 10(4) (85%); Bent over row 10(4) (85%); Shoulder press 10(4) (85%)
SESSION THREE: Run 60mins (RPE 7)

Central YMCA Health and Fitness Guides

5

ENDURANCE

At the start of this chapter it is worth distinguishing between two terms which are commonly seen and used together, cardio and endurance training. For me, a cardio session focuses on maintaining current fitness levels alongside goals such as weight loss or weight maintenance. Endurance training, on the other hand, focuses on improving one's aerobic and/or anaerobic capacity. This endurance chapter therefore looks at ways to increase your ability to run, cycle, row or swim for longer and at a higher intensity.

There are three key outcomes to an effective endurance training programme:

- ☐ An increased aerobic threshold
- ☐ An increased anaerobic threshold
- ☐ Greater utilisation of fat as an energy source

AEROBIC THRESHOLD

Your oxygen consumption rises exponentially during the first few minutes of exercise and consequently endurance training can seem a little uncomfortable until you feel yourself ease into the session. This is essentially because your body takes a short period of time to reach a plateau or a steady state of exercise when there is a balance between the energy required by the working muscles and the ATP production – the currency of energy – being supplied aerobically, that is, in the presence of oxygen.

Aside from things like fluid loss and electrolyte depletion we could theoretically continue forever once we get to steady state exercise. Once we go above this aerobic threshold, however, the aerobic energy production is gradually supported by anaerobic. Lactic acid subsequently accumulates in the blood and muscles causing a level of discomfort which will ultimately affect your performance. Therefore, the longer and quicker you can run under your aerobic threshold, the more success you will have in endurance races. The majority of marathon runners, for example, will be running at this threshold for much of the race to ensure that they can complete it in the best time that they physically can.

FACTORS THAT AFFECT YOUR AEROBIC THRESHOLD

There are five major factors that affect your aerobic threshold:

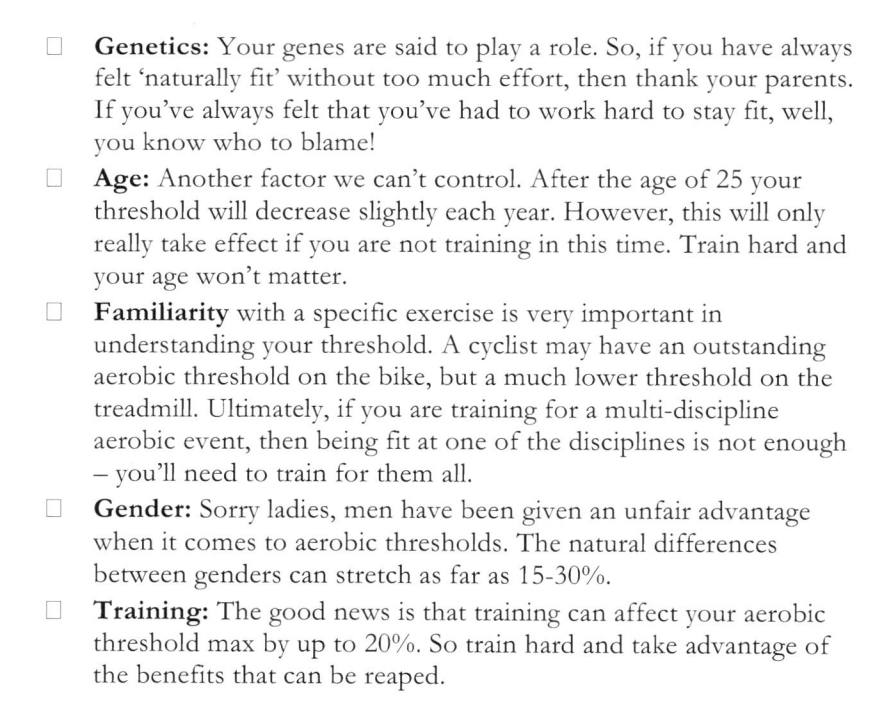

- **Genetics:** Your genes are said to play a role. So, if you have always felt 'naturally fit' without too much effort, then thank your parents. If you've always felt that you've had to work hard to stay fit, well, you know who to blame!
- **Age:** Another factor we can't control. After the age of 25 your threshold will decrease slightly each year. However, this will only really take effect if you are not training in this time. Train hard and your age won't matter.
- **Familiarity** with a specific exercise is very important in understanding your threshold. A cyclist may have an outstanding aerobic threshold on the bike, but a much lower threshold on the treadmill. Ultimately, if you are training for a multi-discipline aerobic event, then being fit at one of the disciplines is not enough – you'll need to train for them all.
- **Gender:** Sorry ladies, men have been given an unfair advantage when it comes to aerobic thresholds. The natural differences between genders can stretch as far as 15-30%.
- **Training:** The good news is that training can affect your aerobic threshold max by up to 20%. So train hard and take advantage of the benefits that can be reaped.

ANAEROBIC THRESHOLD/ONSET OF BLOOD LACTATE ACCUMULATION (OBLA)

Once your aerobic threshold has been reached and lactic acid is entering into your muscles and blood, you will begin to feel some discomfort. If you continue to increase the intensity further, the levels of lactate will be produced faster than the speed at which it can be removed and it will accumulate in the blood. This point is referred to as the anaerobic threshold and is the highest limit of aerobic performance.

It would be foolish to look to complete a long-distance event at just under your anaerobic threshold as the pain and physiological reactions will ultimately cause you to stop. However, shorter distances such as 5-10km races can be completed in or around this threshold. Some of the training programmes in this chapter will require you to work just above and just below your anaerobic threshold. It will be uncomfortable, so why do it? Well, fortunately there are some very notable benefits.

- Training around your anaerobic threshold greatly improves your endurance capabilities.
- Your anaerobic threshold will react faster and more drastically to an effective training programme than your aerobic threshold – offering a more tangible reward for your efforts.
- Adaptations to the cardiovascular system start when working at these intensities.

FAT UTILISATION

As well as the above benefits, there are a number of motivations for undertaking endurance training, with fat loss coming out at the top of the list.

While these training programmes primarily focus on improving fitness and performance, fat loss is a likely added bonus. Aside from the predicted calorie deficit experienced with prolonged endurance training, fat loss can result from the body's utilisation of fat as an energy source.

The human body has a limited amount of energy-supplying carbohydrates in the form of glycogen, but an abundance of fat. Therefore the sooner that fat can be used as the primary energy source, the better.

When it comes to endurance training we are concerned with improving fitness which means working at higher intensities – intensities which invariably require glycogen as a primary energy source. With training, fat will take over as the primary energy source earlier in the session allowing the body to conserve its precious glycogen supplies and the added bonus of fat loss.

TOP TIP

Key to the success of any programme is a steady week-by-week increment. This ensures that the body can adapt at a speed which is manageable and therefore the likelihood of injury is minimised. The devised programmes have taken these principles into account. However, I would also advise that to further minimise the risk of injury, you should incorporate a stretch or core-based session into your weekly schedule. These sessions will help to increase the flexibility of your muscles and joints as well as ensuring that your movement patterns are more aligned and efficient. Try a yoga or supple strength type class at your local fitness centre. It is surprising how quickly you'll see the benefits.

YOUR ENDURANCE TRAINING PROGRAMMES

As always, please make sure that you complete a thorough warm up (as described above) before taking part in any of the sessions in this book.

PROGRAMME 4:
Type of programme: Endurance training – running focused
Level: Entry level fitness programme (perfect for those starting out on their first serious running programme)

Week 1

SESSION ONE: Run 10mins (RPE 6); **Walk** 3mins (2)
SESSION TWO: X-Trainer 20mins (RPE 5-7)
SESSION THREE: Row 500m (RPE 5) (2); **Cycle** 15mins (RPE 7)

Week 2

SESSION ONE: Run 20mins (RPE 6)
SESSION TWO: Squats; Mountain climbers; Lunges; Squat thrusts 20(3); **Row** 1km (RPE 6)
SESSION THREE: Run 20mins (RPE 6)

Week 3

SESSION ONE: Row Continuous 5mins (RPE 5); Interval 15s:45s (RPE 8:4) (8)
SESSION TWO: Run 20mins (RPE 6); **Walk** 2mins; **Run** 10mins (RPE 6)
SESSION THREE: Squats; Mountain climbers; Lunges; Squat thrusts 20(3); **Row** 1km (RPE 6)(2)

Week 4

SESSION ONE: Run Interval 2min:1min (RPE 5:8) 20mins
SESSION TWO: Row Continuous 5mins (RPE 5); Interval 100m:200m (RPE 9:6)(5); **Cycle** 20mins (RPE 7)
SESSION THREE: Run 25mins (RPE 6)

Week 5

SESSION ONE: Row Continuous 5mins (RPE 5); Interval (RPE 10:4)10s:50s; 20s:40s; 30s:30s; 20s:40s; 10s:50s (Rest 1min) (2)
SESSION TWO: Run 30mins (RPE 6)
SESSION THREE: Burpees; Squat jumps; Mountain climbers; Lunges; Squat thrusts 20(3); **Cycle** 10mins (RPE 7)

Week 6

SESSION ONE: Run Interval 75s:45s (RPE 5:9) 20mins
SESSION TWO: Row 1500m; **Cycle** 10km; **Run** 2km (timed)
SESSION THREE: Run 30mins (RPE 7)

Week 7

SESSION ONE: Run Interval 3min:1min (RPE 5:9)(8)
SESSION TWO: Run 40mins (RPE 7)
SESSION THREE: Burpees; Squat jumps; Mountain climbers; Lunges; Squat thrusts 20(3); **Cycle** Interval (RPE 10:4)10s:50s; 20s:40s; 30s:30s; 40s:20s; 50s:10s

Week 8

SESSION ONE: Row Continuous 5mins (RPE 5); Interval (RPE 10:4)10s:50s; 20s:40s; 30s:30s; 40s:20s; 50s:10s (Rest 1min) (2)
SESSION TWO: Row 1500m; **Cycle** 10km; **Run** 2km (timed to beat week 6)
SESSION THREE: Run 45mins (RPE 7)

PROGRAMME 5:

Type of programme: Endurance training
Level: Medium fitness programme (perfect for those who have completed the low fitness programme or anyone who is training for a 5-10km race)

Week 1

SESSION ONE: Run 25mins (RPE 6)
SESSION TWO: Row Continuous 5mins (RPE 5); Interval 100m:150m (RPE 9:6)(5); **Cycle** 15mins (RPE 7)
SESSION THREE: Run 3km: 1km: (RPE 6) rest 2mins; 1km: +0.5km/h from first run rest 2mins; 1km: +1km/h from first run

Week 2

SESSION ONE: Run 30mins (RPE 6)
SESSION TWO: Burpees; Squat jumps; Mountain climbers; Lunges; Squat thrusts 20(3); **Cycle** 20mins
SESSION THREE: Run 30mins (RPE 7)

Week 3

SESSION ONE: Row Continuous 5mins (RPE 5); Interval (RPE 10:4)10s:50s; 20s:40s; 30s:30s; 20s:40s; 10s:50s (Rest 1min) (2)
SESSION TWO: Run 40mins (RPE 6)
SESSION THREE: Burpees; Squat jumps; Mountain climbers; Lunges; Squat thrusts 20(3); **Cycle** Intervals 1min:1min (RPE 9:6) 10mins

Week 4

SESSION ONE: Run Intervals 2min:1min (RPE 5:9) 20mins
SESSION TWO: Row Continuous 5mins (RPE 5); Interval 150m:200m (RPE 9:6)(5); **Cycle** 20mins (RPE 7)
SESSION THREE: Run 40mins (RPE 7)

Week 5

SESSION ONE: Row Continuous 5mins (RPE 5); Interval (RPE 10:4)10s:50s; 20s:40s; 30s:30s; 20s:40s; 10s:50s (Rest 1min) (2)
SESSION TWO: Run 50mins (RPE 7)
SESSION THREE: Burpees; Squat jumps; Mountain climbers; Lunges; Squat thrusts 25(4)

Week 6

SESSION ONE: Run Intervals 2min:1min (RPE 5:9) 30mins
SESSION TWO: Row 2km; **Cycle** 12km; **Run** 3km (timed)
SESSION THREE: Run 50mins (RPE 7)

Week 7

SESSION ONE: Run Intervals 3min:90secs (RPE 5:9) (8)
SESSION TWO: Run 60mins (RPE 7)
SESSION THREE: Burpees; Squat jumps; Mountain climbers; Lunges; Squat thrusts 30(2); **Cycle** 5mins (RPE 8)

Week 8

SESSION ONE: Run 800m; 600m; 400m; 200m; 100m: Rest 150s; 120s; 90s;60s; 180s (2)
SESSION TWO: Row 2km; **Cycle** 12km; **Run** 3km (timed to beat week 6)
SESSION THREE: Run 70mins (RPE 7)

PROGRAMME 6:
Type of programme: Endurance training
Level: High fitness programme (perfect for an experienced runner or those

who are training for a half or full marathon)

Week 1

SESSION ONE: Run 30mins (RPE 6)
SESSION TWO: Row Continuous 5mins (RPE 5); Interval 100m:100m (RPE 9:6)(4); **Cycle** 20mins (RPE 7)
SESSION THREE: Run 3km: 1km: (RPE 6) rest 2mins; 1km: +1km/h from first run rest 2mins; 1km: +2km/h from first run

Week 2

SESSION ONE: Run 30mins (RPE 7)
SESSION TWO: Burpees; Squat jumps; Mountain climbers; Lunges; Squat thrusts 20(3)
SESSION THREE: Run 40mins (RPE 7)

Week 3

SESSION ONE: Row Continuous 5mins (RPE 5); Interval (RPE 10:4)10s:50s; 20s:40s; 30s:30s; 40s:20s; 50s:10s (Rest 1min) (3)
SESSION TWO: Run 40mins (RPE 7)
SESSION THREE: Burpees; Squat jumps; Mountain climbers; Lunges; Squat thrusts (60 of each throughout the session)

Week 4

SESSION ONE: Run Intervals 2mins:1mins (RPE 5:9) 30mins
SESSION TWO: Row Continuous 5mins (RPE 5); Interval 200m:200m (RPE 9:6)(4); **Cycle** 20mins (RPE 7)
SESSION THREE: Run 45mins (RPE 7)

Week 5

SESSION ONE: Row Continuous 5mins (RPE 5); Interval (RPE 10:4)10s:50s; 20s:40s; 30s:30s; 40s:20s; 50s:10s (Rest 1min) (3)
SESSION TWO: Run 50mins (RPE 7)
SESSION THREE: Burpees; Squat jumps; Mountain climbers; Lunges; Squat thrusts (80 of each throughout the session)

Week 6

SESSION ONE: Run Intervals 2min:1min (RPE 5:9) 30mins
SESSION TWO: Row 3km; **Cycle** 15km; **Run** 5km (timed to beat week 6)
SESSION THREE: Run 60mins (RPE 7)

Week 7

SESSION ONE: Run Intervals 2min:2min (RPE 5:9) 40mins
SESSION TWO: Run 75mins (RPE 7)
SESSION THREE: Burpees; Squat jumps; Mountain climbers; Lunges; Squat thrusts (100 of each throughout the session)

Week 8

SESSION ONE: Run 1km; 800m; 600m; 400m; 200m; 100m: Rest 180s; 150s; 120s; 90s;60s; 180s (2)
SESSION TWO: Row 3km; **Cycle** 15km; **Run** 5km (timed to beat week 6)
SESSION THREE: Run 90mins (RPE 7)

PROGRAMME 7:

Type of programme: Endurance training – Triathlon focused
Level: Low fitness programme (perfect for those who are looking to improve their general endurance performance)

Week 1

SESSION ONE: Run 10mins (RPE 6) **Walk** 3mins (2)
SESSION TWO: Row 500m (RPE 5) (2); **Cycle** 15mins (RPE 7)
SESSION THREE: Swim 500m

Week 2

SESSION ONE: Run 20mins (RPE 6)
SESSION TWO: Swim Intervals 100m (8) (RPE 7)
SESSION THREE: Run 20mins (RPE 6)

Week 3

SESSION ONE: Row 750m; **Cycle** 5km (3)
SESSION TWO: Run 25mins (RPE 7)
SESSION THREE: Press ups; Squats; Dumbbell punches (2-4kg); Mountain climbers; Lunges 20(3) (timed)

Week 4

SESSION ONE: Swim Intervals 100m (10) (RPE 8)
SESSION TWO: Row Continuous 5mins (RPE 5); Interval 150m:150m (RPE 9:6)(3); **Cycle** 20mins (RPE 7)
SESSION THREE: Run 30mins (RPE 6)

Week 5

SESSION ONE: Swim 800m
SESSION TWO: Cycle 3km; **Run** 1km (3)
SESSION THREE: Press ups; Squats; Dumbbell punches (2-4kg); Mountain climbers; Lunges 20 (3) (timed to beat week 3 by 1min)

Week 6

SESSION ONE: Run Intervals 2min:1min (RPE 5:9) 25mins
SESSION TWO: Swim 1km
SESSION THREE: Swim 750m; **Cycle** 8km; **Run** 1500m; **Cycle** 4km; **Run** 1500m

Week 7

SESSION ONE: Run Intervals 3min:90s (RPE 5:9) (6)
SESSION TWO: Run 40mins (RPE 6)
SESSION THREE: Press ups; Burpees; Squats; Dumbbell punches (2-4kg); Mountain climbers; Lunges 20(3)

Week 8

SESSION ONE: Run 800m; 600m; 400m; 200m; 100m: Rest 150s; 120s; 90s; 60s; 180s (2)

SESSION TWO: Row 1500m; **Cycle** 12km; **Run** 3km
SESSION THREE: Swim 750m; **Cycle** 10km; **Run** 2km; **Cycle** 5km; **Run** 1km

PROGRAMME 8:

Type of programme: Endurance training
Level: Medium fitness programme (perfect for those who have completed the low level programme or anyone training for their first sprint or Olympic distance triathlon)

Week 1

SESSION ONE: Run 25mins (RPE 6)
SESSION TWO: Row Continuous 5mins (RPE 5); Interval 150m:150m (RPE 9:6)(3); **Cycle** 20mins (RPE 7)
SESSION THREE: Swim 650m

Week 2

SESSION ONE: Run 25mins (RPE 7)
SESSION TWO: Swim Intervals 100m (8) (RPE 8)
SESSION THREE: Run 30mins (RPE 6)

Week 3

SESSION ONE: Cycle 4km; **Run** 1km (3)
SESSION TWO: Run 30mins (RPE 6)
SESSION THREE: Press ups; Burpees; Squats; Dumbbell punches (2-4kg); Mountain climbers; Lunges 15(3)

Week 4

SESSION ONE: Swim Intervals 150m (8) (RPE 8)
SESSION TWO: Row Continuous 5mins (RPE 5); Interval 200m:200m (RPE 9:6)(4); **Cycle** 20mins (RPE 7)
SESSION THREE: Run 35mins (RPE 6)

Week 5

SESSION ONE: Swim 800m

SESSION TWO: Cycle 4km; **Run** 1500m (3)
SESSION THREE: Press ups; Burpees; Squats; Dumbbell punches (2-4kg); Mountain climbers; Lunges 20(3)

Week 6

SESSION ONE: Run Intervals 2min:1min (RPE 5:9) 30mins
SESSION TWO: Swim 1km
SESSION THREE: Swim 750m; **Cycle** 10km; **Run** 2km; **Cycle** 8km; **Run** 1500m

Week 7

SESSION ONE: Run Intervals 3min:90s (RPE 5:9) (8)
SESSION TWO: Run 45mins (RPE 6)
SESSION THREE: Press ups; Burpees; Squats; Dumbbell punches (2-4kg); Mountain climbers; Lunges 25(3)

Week 8

SESSION ONE: Run 800m; 600m; 400m; 200m; 100m: Rest 140s; 100s; 70s; 40s; 140s (2)
SESSION TWO: Row 2km; **Cycle** 12km; **Run** 3km
SESSION THREE: Swim 1km; **Cycle** 10km; **Run** 2km; **Cycle** 10km; **Run** 2km

PROGRAMME 9:

Type of programme: Endurance training – triathlon focused
Level: High fitness programme (perfect for experienced exercisers training to achieve a fast triathlon time)

Week 1

SESSION ONE: Run 30mins (RPE 7)
SESSION TWO: Row Continuous 5mins (RPE 5); Interval 150m:150m (RPE 9:6)(5); **Cycle** 20mins (RPE 7)
SESSION THREE: Swim 800m

Week 2

SESSION ONE: Run 35mins (RPE 7)
SESSION TWO: Swim Intervals 150m (10) (RPE 8)
SESSION THREE: Run 40mins (RPE 7)

Week 3

SESSION ONE: Run 1km; **Cycle** 5km (3)
SESSION TWO: Run 40mins (RPE 7)
SESSION THREE: Press ups; Burpees; Squats; Dumbbell punches (2-4kg); Mountain climbers; Lunges 25(3)

Week 4

SESSION ONE: Swim Intervals 200m (8) (RPE 8)
SESSION TWO: Row Continuous 5mins (RPE 5); Interval 200m:200m (RPE 9:6)(5); **Cycle** 20mins (RPE 7)
SESSION THREE: Run 45mins (RPE 7)

Week 5

SESSION ONE: Swim 1200m
SESSION TWO: Cycle 5km; **Run** 1500m (3)
SESSION THREE: Press ups; Burpees; Squats; Dumbbell punches (2-4kg); Mountain climbers; Lunges 25(3); **Row** 2km

Week 6

SESSION ONE: Run Intervals 90secs:1min (RPE 5:9) 30mins
SESSION TWO: Swim 1200m
SESSION THREE: Swim 1km; **Cycle** 12km; **Run** 3km; **Cycle** 10km; **Run** 2km

Week 7

SESSION ONE: Run Intervals 3min:90s (RPE 5:9) 45mins
SESSION TWO: Run 60mins (RPE 7)
SESSION THREE: Press ups; Burpees; Squats; Dumbbell punches (2-4kg); Mountain climbers; Lunges 25(3); **Row** 1km; **Cycle** 3km

Week 8

SESSION ONE: Run 1km; 800m; 600m; 400m; 200m; 100m: Rest 180s; 140s; 100s; 70s;40s; 140s (2)
SESSION TWO: Row 2km; **Cycle** 12km; **Run** 3km
SESSION THREE: Swim 1km; **Cycle** 12km; **Run** 3km; **Cycle** 12km; **Run** 3km

6

STRENGTH

In days gone by, when free weights rooms or even the concept of gyms were but a mere pipe dream, strongmen would be paraded around at circus events to the amusement of astonished crowds. It seems amazing, particularly when you consider that these men would invariably be no bigger than many members of today's average gym. However, this fascination with strength still exists today and powerlifting, weightlifting, strongman and bodybuilding events remain as popular as ever. The only difference today is that our physical capabilities have increased as a result of diet, science and greater facilities.

The interesting thing about strength training is that whilst so many of us do it, few actually use or follow a programme. Indeed, many simply lift the same weights for the same number of repetitions for years on end, but then endlessly complain that they are seeing no results. The programmes that follow will ensure that this doesn't happen and that you can actually make progress in your strength training.

When performing any weight training, the manipulation of variables such as the number of sets, repetitions, resistance applied and choice of exercise will determine the eventual outcome. This chapter and its associated programmes will focus on strength development and will also look at increasing size.

ADAPTATIONS

It can be frustrating when you train with a partner and their results – particularly aesthetically – are quicker and more effective than yours. You may be working at the same intensity, but your results are different. Why is this?

There are a number of reasons why this could be the case, some of which you are in control of and others that you are not. We all have a range of different muscle fibres (slow twitch, fast twitch type-2a and fast twitch type-2b). Proficient marathon runners will have a higher degree of slow twitch fibres whilst sprinters will have a greater number of fast twitch fibres. Though there can be small alterations through training, these percentages will ultimately remain the same, regardless of the training you do. You can, however, make the best of what you've got by ensuring that the percentage of fast twitch fibres are as efficient and trained as possible. Therefore, following a well-structured programme which challenges you and your muscles in every session will help you to achieve your goals.

NERVOUS SYSTEM

When starting on a weight training programme, your initial strength gains will be quite noticeable, but there may be no visible increase in your muscle mass. This is because neural adaptations play an important role in these dramatic early rises, due to a greater efficiency in neural recruitment patterns, increased central nervous system activation and improved motor unit synchronisation. Put simply, your body's ability to wake up all of its muscle fibres at one time, and to halt the muscles' natural protection mechanisms, will cause these improvements.

MUSCULAR SYSTEM

Whilst neural factors play a part in the early stages of a strength training programme, your ultimate strength capacity depends on the physiological capabilities of your joints and muscles. A strength training programme will increase the size and strength of muscle fibres, and you will see improvements in ligament and tendon strength – together with a decrease in the muscle twitch contraction time. By training with weights that are manageable but challenging to lift, the muscular system triggers signalling proteins that in turn activate the genes to stimulate protein synthesis; thus leading to bigger muscles.

DON'T OVERDO IT!

Another important reason for following a structured programme is to prevent the risk of overtraining, which can ultimately lead to negative effects on your workouts and life. It can be brought on by a variety of factors, such as a sudden increase in training volume, monotonous training, a lack of recovery time and stress levels. Overtraining can cause problems with sleep, reduced ability to perform high intensity exercises and a reduction in general physiological performance. Therefore, no matter how keen you are to get the 'beach body' you dream of, or to get strong in time for the new rugby season, do so in a structured and periodised manner.

TOP TIP

Prior to undertaking your training you will need to establish your maximal levels, which will then enable you to work out the appropriate intensity of your sessions. If you are planning to follow the strength-based sessions then you will need to discover your five-rep-max – the maximum amount of weight that you can lift five times using the appropriate technique. For those focusing on developing their size then you will need to work out your 10-rep-max. You will need to complete this over two sessions in order to get accurate results. I would recommend at least two rest days between these sessions in order to allow for sufficient recovery of the muscles.

YOUR STRENGTH TRAINING PROGRAMMES

To develop strength and/or size, I have put together the following programmes for people with low, medium and high strength levels. These programmes have been devised on the basis that you have previously taken part in exercise and need a structured training programme in order to achieve your goals. Whether you want to develop your strength or build your musculature there will be a programme for you.

As always, please make sure that you complete a thorough warm up (as described above) before taking part in any of the sessions in this book.

PROGRAMME 10:
Type of programme: Strength training – developing absolute strength

Level: Entry level fitness programme (perfect for those who have a low level of weight training experience but are looking to build their strength)

Week 1

SESSION ONE: Squats 10(3) (65%); Deadlift 10(3) (65%); Bench press 10(3) (65%); Bent over row 10(3) (65%); Shoulder press 10(3) (65%)
SESSION TWO: Ab crunches; Plank; Superman; Side plank; Leg drops; Bridge (30secs) (5)
SESSION THREE: Squats 10(3) (65%); Deadlift 10(3) (65%); Bench press 10(3) (65%); Bent over row 10(3) (65%); Shoulder press 10(3) (65%)

Week 2

SESSION ONE: Post exhaust: Bench press; Triceps dips; Lat pulldown; Narrow grip pulldown; Squats; Leg extension; Shoulder press; Prone lat raise 8(4) (80%)
SESSION TWO: Rotator Cuffs: External rotation; Internal rotation; Horizontal abduction; Horizontal adduction; Prone raise; Lat raise; Superman; Bridge; Plank (45secs) (4)
SESSION THREE: Squats 10(3) (70%); Deadlift 10(3) (70%); Bench press 10(3) (70%); Bent over row 10(3) (70%); Shoulder press 10(3) (70%)

Week 3

SESSION ONE: Super sets: DB Shoulder press; Lat raise; Chest flyes; Press ups; Lat pulldown; Single arm row; Biceps curl; Triceps pushdowns 6(4) (80%)
SESSION TWO: Leg extension; Leg curl 8(4) (80%); Lunges; Leg press 6(4) (80%); Calf raises 20(3)
SESSION THREE: Ab crunches; Plank; Superman; Side plank; Leg drops; Bridge (45secs) (5)

Week 4

SESSION ONE: Squats 8(4) (75%); Deadlift 8(4) (75%); Bench press 8(4) (75%); Bent over row 8(4) (75%); Shoulder press 8(4) (75%)
SESSION TWO: Rotator Cuffs: External rotation; Internal rotation; Horizontal abduction; Horizontal adduction; Prone raise; Lat raise; Superman; Bridge; Plank (1min) (4)

SESSION THREE: Pre exhaust: Triceps dips; Bench press; Narrow grip pulldown; Lat pulldown; Leg extension; Squats; Prone lat raise; Shoulder press 8(4) (80%)

Week 5

SESSION ONE: Tri sets: DB Shoulder press; Lat raise; Upright row; Chest flyes; Press ups; Decline bench press; Lat pulldown; Single arm row; Lower back extension 6(3) (85%)
SESSION TWO: Squats 6(4) (85%); Deadlift 6(4) (85%); Bench press 6(4) (85%); Bent over row 6(4) (85%); Shoulder press 6(4) (85%)
SESSION THREE: Ab crunches; Plank; Jack-knifes; Superman; Side plank; Leg drops; Bridge; Weighted crunches (1min) (3)

Week 6

SESSION ONE: Squats 6(4) (85%); Deadlift 6(4) (85%); Bench press 6(4) (85%); Bent over row 6(4) (85%); Shoulder press 6(4) (85%)
SESSION TWO: Leg extension; Leg curl 6(5) (90%); Lunges; Leg press 6(5) (90%); Calf raises 20(3)
SESSION THREE: Super sets: DB Shoulder press; Lat raise; Chest flyes; Press ups; Lat pulldown; Single arm row; Biceps curl; Triceps pushdowns 6(4) (80%)

Week 7

SESSION ONE: Post exhaust: Bench press; Triceps dips; Lat pulldown; Narrow grip pulldown; Squats; Leg extension; Shoulder press; Prone lat raise 6(5) (90%)
SESSION TWO: Squats 6(4) (90%); Deadlift 6(4) (90%); Bench press 6(4) (90%); Bent over row 6(4) (90%); Shoulder press 6(4) (90%)
SESSION THREE: Ab crunches; Plank; Jack-knifes; Superman; Side plank; Leg drops; Bridge; Weighted crunches (1min) (4)

Week 8

SESSION ONE: Squats 6(4) (90%); Deadlift 6(4) (90%); Bench press 6(4) (90%); Bent over row 6(4) (90%); Shoulder press 6(4) (90%)
SESSION TWO: Strip sets: Chest flyes; Lat raise; Bent arm pullover; Biceps curl; Triceps pushdown; Leg press

SESSION THREE: Squats 6(4) (100%); Deadlift 6(4) (100%); Bench press 6(4) (100%); Bent over row 6(4) (100%); Shoulder press 6(4) (100%)

PROGRAMME 11:

Type of programme: Strength training – developing absolute strength
Level: Medium fitness programme (perfect for those who have previously taken part in weight training programmes and wish to develop their strength levels)

Week 1

SESSION ONE: Squats 6(4) (80%); Deadlift 6(4) (80%); Bench press 6(4) (80%); Bent over row 6(4) (80%); Shoulder press 6(4) (80%)
SESSION TWO: Leg extension; Leg curl 6(5) (85%); Lunges; Leg press 6(5) (85%); Calf raises 20(3)
SESSION THREE: Super sets: DB Shoulder press; Lat raise; Chest flyes; Press ups; Lat pulldown; Single arm row; Biceps curl; Triceps pushdowns 6(4) (80%)

Week 2

SESSION ONE: Post exhaust: Bench press; Triceps dips; Lat pulldown; Narrow grip pulldown; Squats; Leg extension; Shoulder press; Prone lat raise 6(5) (85%)
SESSION TWO: Squats 6(4) (85%); Deadlift 6(4) (85%); Bench press 6(4) (85%); Bent over row 6(4) (85%); Shoulder press 6(4) (85%)
SESSION THREE: Ab crunches; Plank; Jack-knifes; Superman; Side plank; Leg drops; Bridge; Weighted crunches (1min) (4)

Week 3

SESSION ONE: Squats 6(4) (85%); Deadlift 6(4) (85%); Bench press 6(4) (85%); Bent over row 6(4) (85%); Shoulder press 6(4) (85%)
SESSION TWO: Rotator Cuffs: External rotation; Internal rotation; Horizontal abduction; Horizontal adduction; Prone raise; Lat raise; Superman; Bridge; Plank (1min) (4)
SESSION THREE: Bench press 6(4) (90%); Chest flyes 6(4) (90%); Triceps pushdown 6(4) (90%); Incline chest press 6(3) (90%); Triceps

extension 6(4) (90%)

Week 4

SESSION ONE: Tri sets: DB Shoulder press; Lat raise; Upright row; Chest flyes; Press ups; Decline bench press; Lat pulldown; Single arm row; Lower back extension 6(4) (90%)
SESSION TWO: Squats 6(4) (90%); Deadlift 6(4) (90%); Bench press 6(4) (90%); Bent over row 6(4) (90%); Shoulder press 6(4) (90%)
SESSION THREE: Ab crunches; Plank; Jack-knifes; Superman; Side plank; Leg drops; Bridge; Weighted crunches (1min) (4)

Week 5

SESSION ONE: Lat Pulldown 6(3) (85%); Deadlift 6(3) (85%); Single arm row 6(3) (85%); Upright row 6(3) (85%); Shoulder press 6(3) (85%); Lat raise 6(3) (85%); Biceps curl 6(3) (85%); Hammer curl 6(3) (85%)
SESSION TWO: Rotator Cuffs: External rotation; Internal rotation; Horizontal abduction; Horizontal adduction; Prone raise; Lat raise; Superman; Bridge; Plank (1min) (5)
SESSION THREE: Leg extension; Leg curl 6(5) (90%); Lunges; Leg press 6(5) (90%); Calf raises 20(3)

Week 6

SESSION ONE: Post exhaust: Bench press; Triceps dips; Lat pulldown; Narrow grip pulldown; Squats; Leg extension; Shoulder press; Prone lat raise 6(5) (95%)
SESSION TWO: Squats 6(4) (95%); Deadlift 6(4) (95%); Bench press 6(4) (95%); Bent over row 6(4) (95%); Shoulder press 6(4) (95%)
SESSION THREE: Giant sets: Chest flyes; Press ups; Decline bench press; Incline bench press; Shoulder press; Lat raise; Upright row; Prone raise; Lat pulldown; Single arm row; Pull ups; Bent arm pullover 5(3) (95%)

Week 7

SESSION ONE: Lat Pulldown 6(3) (90%); Deadlift 6(3) (90%); Single arm row 6(3) (90%); Upright row 6(3) (90%); Shoulder press 6(3) (90%); Lat raise 6(3) (90%); Biceps curl 6(3) (90%); Hammer curl 6(3) (90%)
SESSION TWO: Bench press 6(4) (95%); Chest flyes 6(4) (95%); Triceps

pushdown 6(4) (95%); Incline chest press 6(3) (95%); Triceps extension 6(4) (95%)
SESSION THREE: Leg extension; Leg curl 6(5) (95%); Lunges; Leg press 6(5) (95%); Calf raises 20(3)

Week 8

SESSION ONE: Squats 6(4) (100%); Deadlift 6(4) (100%); Bench press 6(4) (100%); Bent over row 6(4) (100%); Shoulder press 6(4) (100%)
SESSION TWO: Strip sets: Chest flyes; Lat raise; Bent arm pullover; Biceps curl; Triceps pushdown; Leg press
SESSION THREE: Squats 6(4) (100%); Deadlift 6(4) (100%); Bench press 6(4) (100%); Bent over row 6(4) (100%); Shoulder press 6(4) (100%)

PROGRAMME 12:

Type of programme: Strength training – developing absolute strength
Level: High fitness programme (perfect for those who have completed the medium fitness programme or those looking to build strength for performance improvements in sports or weight-lifting competitions)

Week 1

SESSION ONE: Squats 6(4) (85%); Deadlift 6(4) (85%); Bench press 6(4) (85%); Bent over row 6(4) (85%); Shoulder press 6(4) (85%)
SESSION TWO: Leg extension; Leg curl 6(5) (90%); Lunges; Leg press 6(5) (90%); Calf raises 20(3)
SESSION THREE: DB Shoulder press; Lat raise; Upright row; Chest flyes; Press ups; Decline bench press; Lat pulldown; Single arm row; Lower back extension 6(4) (85%)

Week 2

SESSION ONE: Post exhaust: Bench press; Triceps dips; Lat pulldown; Narrow grip pulldown; Squats; Leg extension; Shoulder press; Prone lat raise 5(6) (95%)
SESSION TWO: Squats 6(4) (90%); Deadlift 6(4) (90%); Bench press 6(4) (90%); Bent over row 6(4) (90%); Shoulder press 6(4) (90%)

SESSION THREE: Ab crunches; Plank; Jackknifes; Superman; Side plank; Leg drops; Bridge; Weighted crunches (1min) (4)

Week 3

SESSION ONE: Lat Pulldown 6(3) (90%); Deadlift 6(3) (90%); Single arm row 6(3) (90%); Upright row 6(3) (90%); Shoulder press 6(3) (90%); Lat raise 6(3) (90%); Biceps curl 6(3) (90%); Hammer curl 6(3) (90%)
SESSION TWO: Bench press 6(4) (90%); Chest flyes 6(4) (90%); Triceps pushdown 6(4) (90%); Incline chest press 6(3) (90%); Triceps extension 6(4) (90%)
SESSION THREE: Leg extension; Leg curl 6(5) (90%); Lunges; Leg press 6(5) (90%); Calf raises 20(3)

Week 4

SESSION ONE: Post exhaust: Bench press; Triceps dips; Lat pulldown; Narrow grip pulldown; Squats; Leg extension; Shoulder press; Prone lat raise 5(4) (100%)
SESSION TWO: Squats 6(4) (95%); Deadlift 6(4) (95%); Bench press 6(4) (95%); Bent over row 6(4) (95%); Shoulder press 6(4) (95%)
SESSION THREE: Giant sets: Chest flyes; Press ups; Decline bench press; Incline bench press; Shoulder press; Lat raise; Upright row; Prone raise; Lat pulldown; Single arm row; Pull ups; Bent arm pullover 5(3) (90%)

Week 5

SESSION ONE: Squats 6(4) (95%); Deadlift 6(4) (95%); Bench press 6(4) (95%); Bent over row 6(4) (95%); Shoulder press 6(4) (95%)
SESSION TWO: Strip sets: Chest flyes; Lat raise; Bent arm pullover; Biceps curl; Triceps pushdown; Leg press
SESSION THREE: Ab crunches; Plank; Jack-knifes; Superman; Side plank; Leg drops; Bridge; Weighted crunches (1min) (5)

Week 6

SESSION ONE: Lat Pulldown 6(3) (95%); Deadlift 6(3) (95%); Single arm row 6(3) (95%); Upright row 6(3) (95%); Shoulder press 6(3) (95%); Lat raise 6(3) (95%); Biceps curl 6(3) (95%); Hammer curl 6(3) (95%)
SESSION TWO: Bench press 6(4) (90%); Chest flyes 6(4) (90%); Triceps

pushdown 6(4) (90%); Incline chest press 6(3) (90%); Triceps extension 6(4) (90%)
SESSION THREE: Leg extension; Leg curl 6(5) (95%); Lunges; Leg press 6(5) (95%); Calf raises 20(3)

Week 7

SESSION ONE: Squats 6(4) (100%); Deadlift 6(4) (100%); Bench press 6(4) (100%); Bent over row 6(4) (100%); Shoulder press 6(4) (100%)
SESSION TWO: Ab crunches; Plank; Jack-knifes; Superman; Side plank; Leg drops; Bridge; Weighted crunches (1min) (5)
SESSION THREE: Squats 6(4) (100%); Deadlift 6(4) (100%); Bench press 6(4) (100%); Bent over row 6(4) (100%); Shoulder press 6(4) (100%)

Week 8

SESSION ONE: Squats 6(4) (110%); Deadlift 6(4) (110%); Bench press 6(4) (110%); Bent over row 6(4) (110%); Shoulder press 6(4) (110%)
SESSION TWO: Strip sets: Chest flyes; Lat raise; Bent arm pullover; Biceps curl; Triceps pushdown; Leg press
SESSION THREE: Squats 6(4) (110%); Deadlift 6(4) (110%); Bench press 6(4) (110%); Bent over row 6(4) (110%); Shoulder press 6(4) (110%)

PROGRAMME 13:
Type of programme: Strength training – size development
Level: Low fitness programme (perfect for perfect for those who have a low level of weight training experience but are looking to build their size)

Week 1

SESSION ONE: Squats 10(3) (60%); Deadlift 10(3) (60%); Bench press 10(3) (60%); Bent over row 10(3) (60%); Shoulder press 10(3) (60%)
SESSION TWO: Ab crunches; Plank; Superman; Side plank; Leg drops; Bridge (40secs) (5)
SESSION THREE: Squats 10(3) (65%); Deadlift 10(3) (65%); Bench press 10(3) (65%); Bent over row 10(3) (65%); Shoulder press 10(3) (65%)

Week 2

SESSION ONE: Post exhaust: Bench press; Triceps dips; Lat pulldown; Narrow grip pulldown; Squats; Leg extension; Shoulder press; Prone lat raise 10(4) (65%)
SESSION TWO: Rotator Cuffs: External rotation; Internal rotation; Horizontal abduction; Horizontal adduction; Prone raise; Lat raise; Superman; Bridge; Plank (45secs) (4)
SESSION THREE: Squats 10(3) (70%); Deadlift 10(3) (70%); Bench press 10(3) (70%); Bent over row 10(3) (70%); Shoulder press 10(3) (70%)

Week 3

SESSION ONE: Super sets: DB Shoulder press; Lat raise; Chest flyes; Press ups; Lat pulldown; Single arm row; Biceps curl; Triceps pushdowns 8(4) (75%)
SESSION TWO: Leg extension; Leg curl 10(4) (75%); Lunges; Leg press 10(4) (75%); Calf raises 20(3)
SESSION THREE: Ab crunches; Plank; Superman; Side plank; Leg drops; Bridge (45secs) (5)

Week 4

SESSION ONE: Squats 8(4) (75%); Deadlift 8(4) (75%); Bench press 8(4) (75%); Bent over row 8(4) (75%); Shoulder press 8(4) (75%)
SESSION TWO: Rotator Cuffs: External rotation; Internal rotation; Horizontal abduction; Horizontal adduction; Prone raise; Lat raise; Superman; Bridge; Plank (1min) (4)
SESSION THREE: Pre exhaust: Triceps dips; Bench press; Narrow grip pulldown; Lat pulldown; Leg extension; Squats; Prone lat raise; Shoulder press 12(3) (75%)

Week 5

SESSION ONE: Tri sets: DB Shoulder press; Lat raise; Upright row; Chest flyes; Press ups; Decline bench press; Lat pulldown; Single arm row; Lower back extension 8(4) (80%)
SESSION TWO: Squats 10(4) (85%); Deadlift 10(4) (85%); Bench press 10(4) (85%); Bent over row 10(4) (85%); Shoulder press 10(4) (85%)
SESSION THREE: Ab crunches; Plank; Jack-knifes; Superman; Side

plank; Leg drops; Bridge; Weighted crunches (1min) (3)

Week 6

SESSION ONE: Squats 8(4) (85%); Deadlift 8(4) (85%); Bench press 8(4) (85%); Bent over row 8(4) (85%); Shoulder press 8(4) (85%)
SESSION TWO: Leg extension; Leg curl 10(4) (90%); Lunges; Leg press 10(4) (90%); Calf raises 20(3)
SESSION THREE: Super sets: DB Shoulder press; Lat raise; Chest flyes; Press ups; Lat pulldown; Single arm row; Biceps curl; Triceps pushdowns 10(4) (85%)

Week 7

SESSION ONE: Post exhaust: Bench press; Triceps dips; Lat pulldown; Narrow grip pulldown; Squats; Leg extension; Shoulder press; Prone lat raise 12(3) (90%)
SESSION TWO: Squats 10(5) (90%); Deadlift 10(5) (90%); Bench press 10(5) (90%); Bent over row 10(5) (90%); Shoulder press 10(5) (90%)
SESSION THREE: Ab crunches; Plank; Jack-knifes; Superman; Side plank; Leg drops; Bridge; Weighted crunches (1min) (4)

Week 8

SESSION ONE: Squats 10(5) (95%); Deadlift 10(5) (95%); Bench press 10(5) (95%); Bent over row 10(5) (95%); Shoulder press 10(5) (95%)
SESSION TWO: Strip sets: Chest flyes; Lat raise; Bent arm pullover; Biceps curl; Triceps pushdown; Leg press
SESSION THREE: Squats 6(4) (100%); Deadlift 6(4) (100%); Bench press 6(4) (100%); Bent over row 6(4) (100%); Shoulder press 6(4) (100%)

PROGRAMME 14:

Type of programme: Strength training – size development
Level: Medium fitness programme (perfect for those who have previously taken part in weight training programmes and wish to develop their muscular size)

Week 1

SESSION ONE: Squats 10(3) (65%); Deadlift 10(3) (65%); Bench press 10(3) (65%); Bent over row 10(3) (65%); Shoulder press 10(3) (65%)
SESSION TWO: Leg extension; Leg curl 10(4) (80%); Lunges; Leg press 10(4) (80%); Calf raises 20(3)
SESSION THREE: Super sets: DB Shoulder press; Lat raise; Chest flyes; Press ups; Lat pulldown; Single arm row; Biceps curl; Triceps pushdowns 12(3) (75%)

Week 2

SESSION ONE: Post exhaust: Bench press; Triceps dips; Lat pulldown; Narrow grip pulldown; Squats; Leg extension; Shoulder press; Prone lat raise 10(4) (75%)
SESSION TWO: Squats 10(3) (70%); Deadlift 10(3) (70%); Bench press 10(3) (70%); Bent over row 10(3) (70%); Shoulder press 10(3) (70%)
SESSION THREE: Ab crunches; Plank; Superman; Side plank; Leg drops; Bridge (45secs) (5)

Week 3

SESSION ONE: Squats 12(3) (70%); Deadlift 12(3) (70%); Bench press 12(3) (70%); Bent over row 12(3) (70%); Shoulder press 12(3) (70%)
SESSION TWO: Rotator Cuffs: External rotation; Internal rotation; Horizontal abduction; Horizontal adduction; Prone raise; Lat raise; Superman; Bridge; Plank (1min) (4)
SESSION THREE: Bench press 8(4) (85%); Chest flyes 8(4) (85%); Triceps pushdown 8(4) (85%); Incline chest press 8(3) (85%); Triceps extension 8(3) (85%)

Week 4

SESSION ONE: Tri sets: DB Shoulder press; Lat raise; Upright row; Chest flyes; Press ups; Decline bench press; Lat pulldown; Single arm row; Lower back extension 8(4) (85%)
SESSION TWO: Squats 10(4) (80%); Deadlift 10(4) (80%); Bench press 10(4) (80%); Bent over row 10(4) (80%); Shoulder press 10(4) (80%)
SESSION THREE: Ab crunches; Plank; Superman; Side plank; Leg drops; Bridge; Decline weighted crunches (1min) (4)

Week 5

SESSION ONE: Lat Pulldown 8(5) (85%); Deadlift 8(5) (85%); Single arm row 8(5) (85%); Upright row 8(5) (85%); Shoulder press 8(5) (85%); Lat raise 8(5) (85%); Biceps curl 8(5) (85%); Hammer curl 8(5) (85%)
SESSION TWO: Rotator Cuffs: External rotation; Internal rotation; Horizontal abduction; Horizontal adduction; Prone raise; Lat raise; Superman; Bridge; Plank (1min) (4)
SESSION THREE: Leg extension; Leg curl 10(4) (90%); Lunges; Leg press 10(4) (90%); Calf raises 20(3)

Week 6

SESSION ONE: Post exhaust: Bench press; Triceps dips; Lat pulldown; Narrow grip pulldown; Squats; Leg extension; Shoulder press; Prone lat raise 10(4) (90%)
SESSION TWO: Ascending pyramids: Bench Press; Lat Pulldown; Shoulder Press; Squats; Biceps curl; Triceps pushdown; 15(60%); 12(70%); 10(75%); 8(85%); 5(90%)
SESSION THREE: Giant sets: DB Shoulder press; Lat raise; Upright row; Prone raise**;** Chest flyes**;** Press ups; Decline chest press; Incline chest press; Lat pulldown; Single arm row; Pull ups; Bent arm pullover 10(4) (90%)

Week 7

SESSION ONE: Lat Pulldown 8(5) (90%); Deadlift 8(5) (90%); Single arm row 8(5) (90%); Upright row 8(5) (90%); Shoulder press 8(5) (90%); Lat raise 8(5) (90%); Biceps curl 8(5) (90%); Hammer curl 8(5) (90%)
SESSION TWO: Bench press 8(5) (90%); Chest flyes 8(5) (90%); Triceps pushdown 8(5) (90%); Incline chest press 8(5) (90%); Triceps extension 8(5) (90%)
SESSION THREE: Leg extension; Leg curl 10(4) (100%); Lunges; Leg press 10(4) (100%); Calf raises 20(3)

Week 8

SESSION ONE: Squats 10(5) (100%); Deadlift 10(5) (100%); Bench press 10(5) (100%); Bent over row 10(5) (100%); Shoulder press 10(5) (100%)
SESSION TWO: Strip sets: Chest flyes**;** Lat raise**;** Bent arm pullover;

Biceps curl; Triceps pushdown; Leg press
SESSION THREE: Ascending pyramids: Bench Press; Lat Pulldown; Shoulder Press; Squats; Biceps curl; Triceps pushdown; 15(60%); 12(70%); 10(75%); 8(85%); 5(95%)

PROGRAMME 15:

Type of programme: Strength training
Level: High fitness programme (perfect for those who have completed the medium fitness programme or those looking to build significant muscle size to their appearance)

Week 1

SESSION ONE: Squats 10(3) (70%); Deadlift 10(3) (70%); Bench press 10(3) (70%); Bent over row 10(3) (70%); Shoulder press 10(3) (70%)
SESSION TWO: Leg extension; Leg curl 12(4) (80%); Lunges; Leg press 10(4) (80%); Calf raises 20(3)
SESSION THREE: Super sets: DB Shoulder press; Lat raise; Chest flyes; Press ups; Lat pulldown; Single arm row; Biceps curl; Triceps pushdowns 12(3) (75%)

Week 2

SESSION ONE: Post exhaust: Bench press; Triceps dips; Lat pulldown; Narrow grip pulldown; Squats; Leg extension; Shoulder press; Prone lat raise 8(5) (80%)
SESSION TWO: Squats 10(3) (75%); Deadlift 10(3) (75%); Bench press 10(3) (75%); Bent over row 10(3) (75%); Shoulder press 10(3) (75%)
SESSION THREE: Ab crunches; Plank; Superman; Side plank; Leg drops; Single leg bridge; Weighted crunches (1min) (5)

Week 3

SESSION ONE: Tri sets: DB Shoulder press; Lat raise; Upright row; Chest flyes; Press ups; Decline bench press; Lat pulldown; Single arm row; Lower back extension 8(4) (85%)
SESSION TWO: Rotator Cuffs: External rotation; Internal rotation; Horizontal abduction; Horizontal adduction; Prone raise; Lat raise;

Superman; Bridge; Plank (1min) (4)
SESSION THREE: Bench press 8(4) (85%); Chest flyes 8(4) (85%); Triceps pushdown 8(4) (85%); Incline chest press 8(4) (85%); Triceps extension 8(4) (85%)

Week 4

SESSION ONE: Post exhaust: Bench press; Triceps dips; Lat pulldown; Narrow grip pulldown; Squats; Leg extension; Shoulder press; Prone lat raise 10(4) (90%)
SESSION TWO: Ascending pyramids: Bench Press; Lat Pulldown; Shoulder Press; Squats; Biceps curl; Triceps pushdown; 15(60%); 12(70%); 10(75%); 8(85%); 5(95%)
SESSION THREE: Ab crunches; Plank; Superman; Side plank; Leg drops; Bridge; Decline weighted crunches (1min) (4)

Week 5

SESSION ONE: Lat Pulldown 8(5) (90%); Deadlift 8(5) (90%); Single arm row 8(5) (90%); Upright row 8(5) (90%); Shoulder press 8(5) (90%); Lat raise 8(5) (90%); Biceps curl 8(5) (90%); Hammer curl 8(5) (90%)
SESSION TWO: Strip sets: Chest flyes; Lat raise; Bent arm pullover; Biceps curl; Triceps pushdown; Leg press
SESSION THREE: Leg extension; Leg curl 12(4) (90%); Lunges; Leg press 12(4) (90%); Calf raises 20(3)

Week 6

SESSION ONE: Squats 10(10) (85%); Bench press 10(10) (85%); Bent over row 10(10) (85%)
SESSION TWO: Ascending pyramids: Bench Press; Lat Pulldown; Shoulder Press; Squats; Biceps curl; Triceps pushdown; 15(60%); 12(70%); 10(75%); 8(85%); 5(90%)
SESSION THREE: Giant sets: DB Shoulder press; Lat raise; Upright row; Prone raise; Chest flyes; Press ups; Decline chest press; Incline chest press; Lat pulldown; Single arm row; Pull ups; Bent arm pullover 10(4) (90%)

Week 7

SESSION ONE: Lat Pulldown 8(5) (95%); Deadlift 8(5) (95%); Single arm row 8(5) (95%); Upright row 8(5) (95%); Shoulder press 8(5) (95%); Lat raise 8(5) (95%); Biceps curl 8(5) (95%); Hammer curl 8(5) (95%)
SESSION TWO: Bench press 8(5) (95%); Chest flyes 8(5) (95%); Triceps pushdown 8(5) (95%); Incline chest press 8(5) (95%); Triceps extension 8(5) (95%)
SESSION THREE: Leg extension; Leg curl 10(5) (100%); Lunges; Leg press 10(5) (100%); Calf raises 20(3)

Week 8

SESSION ONE: Squats 10(5) (100%); Deadlift 10(5) (100%); Bench press 10(5) (100%); Bent over row 10(5) (100%); Shoulder press 10(5) (100%)
SESSION TWO: Strip sets: Chest flyes; Lat raise; Bent arm pullover; Biceps curl; Triceps pushdown; Leg press
SESSION THREE: Full pyramids: Bench Press; Lat Pulldown; Shoulder Press; Squats; Biceps curl; Triceps pushdown; 12(80%); 10(90%); 8(100%); 4(110%); 8(100%); 10(90%);12(80%)

Central YMCA Health and Fitness Guides

7

POWER

Power plays a pivotal role in the vast majority of sports. Generally, if developing power is a key goal for you, the likelihood is that you will be looking to gain a specific performance improvement, be it to increase your jumping ability, sprint speed or explosive strength. This chapter will offer you some key training principles to achieve these goals.

The training programmes below have deliberately focused on developing power as an entity across the body as opposed to only on specific lifts.

WHAT DO WE MEAN BY POWER?

A power-orientated exercise involves an acceleration occurring throughout the whole range of the movement, thus resulting in higher movement speeds and subsequent higher power outputs, simply illustrated by the following equation:

Power = force x velocity

Essentially this means that power is a perfect combination of strength and speed. With this in mind, it seems mystifying that many training programmes focus solely on developing raw strength as a way to generate power. I agree that strength is fundamentally 50% of the contribution to power, but if you completely ignore the other 50% – speed – then your level of success is likely to be limited.

Jonathan Edwards, who still holds the world record for the triple jump with a staggering 18.29m (recorded in Gothenburg, Sweden in 1995), was not massively muscle-bound but combined speed and strength to maximal effect to achieve an amazing record in a sport that epitomises power.

PLYOMETRICS

Plyometric exercises (quick, powerful movements that involve a pre-stretching or countermovement that enables activation of the stretch-shortening cycle) aim to link absolute strength and speed of movement to produce explosive reactive movements and should therefore form a key part of your power-based sessions.

The stretch-shortening cycle referred to above is a clever mechanism that utilises the effects of the energy storage abilities of the muscle to produce a powerful movement over as short a time as possible. The series elastic component of the muscle is responsible for the stretch-shortening cycle. It works by acting, as its name suggests, as an elastic bundle of energy.

MOVEMENT PHASES

During most movements there are three distinct phases:

1. An eccentric phase: The lowering phase of an exercise whereby the muscles are lengthening under tension.
2. The amortisation phase: A transition movement which involves dynamic stabilisation of the muscle under tension.
3. The concentric phase: When the muscle shortens in length to perform the movement.

To describe the key principle of plyometric training, let's examine a squat. In the eccentric phase, on the downwards part of the squat, the series elastic component of the quadriceps and hamstrings are lengthened and they store all of the elastic energy that has been generated. This energy will be used during the concentric part of the squat when attempting to return to fully upright from the lowered position. The key element in how much of this elastic energy can be used for the concentric part is decided by the length of the middle phase – the amortisation phase. The quicker this period in the middle is completed, the more energy is available for the concentric phase. The take home message is: when training for power, perform movements at the maximal speed possible and focus on limiting the time between the muscle lengthening and shortening. Imagine an elastic band, pull it back as far as possible and release it immediately, and it'll go a lot further than if you pull it back and slowly release it bit by bit. Your muscles are the same.

If you accompany a well-structured plyometric programme with strength training, you are likely to get a significant increase in your power output. Yet it is important to pinpoint the intensity of the strength training to avoid causing a detrimental effect.

THE IMPORTANCE OF SPEED

As discussed, the speed of movement is vital in power exercises. Imagine lifting a weight that is between 90-95% of your one-rep-max. How quickly will you perform this? It's fair to say that it is unlikely to be in the region of 300ms, which is indicative of a power-based exercise; in fact you are looking at between 1-2 seconds for the concentric phase, leading to your neuromuscular system training at a speed which could be up to four times slower than required in a typical power-based movement. In terms of specificity, this is too great a discrepancy.

If you are looking at completing a power-based training programme in order to look more muscular, then I'd advise caution. With any resistance programme that is performed at a high intensity, there is likely to be some element of muscle growth, but in the programmes I've devised, the aim is to improve the efficiency of the muscle as opposed to the size.

Explosive strength training leads to specific neural adaptations, including an increased rate of motor unit activation by synchronising the fast twitch motor units to collectively fire at the same time. For a muscular contraction to take place effectively, we need as many of our motor units in our muscles to work together to produce a movement. It is effectively the difference between going into battle with 70% of your soldiers or 100%. Which is more likely to be successful?

The combination of strength training and plyometrics has been found to increase power significantly. Weight training at 65% of one-rep-max has been viewed as an effective figure to generate an optimum development. As such, the training programmes below have incorporated both of these approaches.

As a note of caution, however, plyometric training puts notable strain upon the joints and will likely cause delayed onset of muscle soreness (DOMS). Regardless of your general fitness levels, if you have never trained for power before, I'd strongly advise that you begin at the low level programme until you build up your tolerance to the demands of this mixed modality training.

TOP TIP

For power-based sessions, I would advise caution when selecting your programme. Don't assume that if you would classify yourself as fairly fit then you should immediately attempt the medium or high level programme. Power-based sessions will make your muscles work and react in ways they may be unaccustomed to without previous explosive training. Don't be too ambitious. If you're unsure, try week one of the low level sessions and then make your decision after that.

THE PROGRAMMES

In comparison to the other programmes developed for this book, power is likely to be the area that most people would have focused on the least in the past. Power-based exercises are not as prevalent in fitness environments and, as I discussed earlier, many people misconstrue a strength-based session for a power-based one.

In preparation for some of the resistance elements of the programmes, you will have to establish your 10-rep-max. Please refer to the strength chapter which gives more information on which exercises this applies to.

Remember, for power sessions, it is important to perform all activities with maximal effort and limited time between the eccentric and concentric phases. Therefore expect to feel tired during the sessions.

YOUR POWER TRAINING PROGRAMMES

PROGRAMME 16:
Type of programme: Power training
Level: Entry level fitness programme (perfect for experienced exercisers who wish to add power to their sporting or gym performance)

Week 1

SESSION ONE: High knee jogging; Lunge into high knee; Side to side ankle hops ; Standing jump and reach ; Front cone hops 15 (3) Low intensity

SESSION TWO: Squats 10(3) (65%); Deadlift 10(3) (65%); Bench press 10(3) (65%); Bent over row 10(3) (65%); Shoulder press 10(3) (65%)
SESSION THREE: Tuck Jumps; Squat jumps 15(4); Skipping 1min (3); Squats; Lunges; Calf raises 12(4) (65%); Run 500m(2)(RPE 8)

Week 2

SESSION ONE: Squat jumps; Lateral jumps; Power skipping; Vertical jump; Burpees 15(4)
SESSION TWO: High knee jogging; Lunge into high knee; Side to side ankle hops ; Standing jump and reach ; Front cone hops 15 (3) Medium intensity
SESSION THREE: Squats 8(4) (80%); Deadlift 8(4) (80%); Bench press 8(4) (80%); Bent over row 10(3) (70%); Shoulder press 10(3) (70%)

Week 3

SESSION ONE: MB trunk rotation 10; MB throw 10; MB bounce 10; DB punches (2-4kg) 30s; Burpees 20; (5)
SESSION TWO: Squats 6(5) (80%); Deadlift 6(5) (80%); Bench press 6(5) (80%); Bent over row 6(5) (80%); Shoulder press 6(5) (80%)
SESSION THREE: Cycle 500m (10) (RPE 9); **Row** 100m (8) (RPE 9)

Week 4

SESSION ONE: Squat jumps; Lateral jumps; Power skipping; Vertical jump; Burpees 10(6)
SESSION TWO: Row 100m (10) (RPE 10); **Run** 20s (10) (RPE 10)
SESSION THREE: Push press 15(3) (60%); Bench press 10(4)(65%); Bent over row 10(4) (65%); Deadlift 8(5)(65%)

Week 5

SESSION ONE: Squats 5 (80%); Squat jumps 10; Lunges 5 (80%); Lunge jumps 10; (3); Falling starts and sprint 30m (8)
SESSION TWO: Push press 15(3) (60%); Bench press 10(4)(65%); Bent over row 10(4) (65%); Deadlift 10(4)(65%)
SESSION THREE: Row 100m (10) (RPE 10); **Run** 30s (10) (RPE 10)

Week 6

SESSION ONE: Bench press 5 (85%); MB press 10 (4); Lat Pulldown 5 (85%); MBl bounce 10 (4); Shoulder press 5 (85%); MB throw 10 (4)
SESSION TWO: Skipping 1min (3); Tuck jumps 10; Squat jumps 10; Bounding 20m; Vertical jumps 10; Lateral obstacle jumps 10; (4)
SESSION THREE: Push press 15(3) (60%); Bench press 10(4)(65%); Bent over row 10(4) (65%); Deadlift 10(4)(65%); Cleans 8(3) (60%)

Week 7

SESSION ONE: Row 150m (10) (RPE 10); **Run** 30s (10) (RPE 10)
SESSION TWO: Clap press ups 10; MB trunk rotation 10; MB throw 10; MB bounce 10; DB punches (2-4kg) 30s; Burpees 20; (5)
SESSION THREE: Skipping 1min (3); Tuck jumps 10; Squat jumps 10; Bounding 20m; Vertical jumps 10; Lateral obstacle jumps 10; (5)

Week 8

SESSION ONE: Squats 6 (90%); Squat jumps 15; Lunges 6 (90%); Lunge jumps 10; Calf raises 20; Vertical jumps 10; (5); Falling starts and sprint 30m (10)
SESSION TWO: Push press 15(3) (60%); Bench press 10(4)(65%); Bent over row 10(4) (65%); Deadlift 10(4)(65%); Cleans 8(3) (60%)
SESSION THREE: Row Continuous 5mins (RPE 5); Interval 150m:150m (RPE 9:6)(5); **Cycle** 10mins (RPE 8)

PROGRAMME 17:
Type of programme: Power training
Level: Medium fitness programme (perfect for those who have previously taken part in power sessions and are looking to build upon this for their sporting performance)

Week 1

SESSION ONE: Squat jumps; Lateral jumps; Power skipping; Vertical jumps; Burpees (60 of each in total throughout the session)
SESSION TWO: High knee jogging; Lunge into high knee; Side to side ankle hops ; Standing jump and reach ; Front cone hops 15 (3) Medium

intensity
SESSION THREE: Squats 8(5) (80%); Deadlift 8(5) (80%); Bench press 8(5) (80%); Bent over row 10(3) (70%); Shoulder press 10(3) (70%)

Week 2

SESSION ONE: MB trunk rotation 15; MB throw 15; MB bounce 15; DB punches (2-4kg) 45s; Burpees 20; (6)
SESSION TWO: Squats 6(6) (85%); Deadlift 6(6) (85%); Bench press 6(6) (85%); Bent over row 8(5) (80%); Shoulder press 8(5) (80%)
SESSION THREE: Cycle 500m (10) (RPE 9); **Row** 150m (8) (RPE 9)

Week 3

SESSION ONE: Squat jumps; Lateral jumps; Power skipping; Vertical jumps; Burpees (75 of each in total throughout the session)
SESSION TWO: Row 150m (10) (RPE 10); **Run** 30s (10) (RPE 10)
SESSION THREE: Push press 10(4) (70%); Bench press 10(4)(70%); Bent over row 10(4) (70%); Deadlift 10(4)(70%); Cleans 8(3) (60%)

Week 4

SESSION ONE: Squats 6 (90%); Squat jumps 15; Lunges 6 (90%); Lunge jumps 10; Calf raises 20; Vertical jumps 10; (5); Falling starts and sprint 30m (10)
SESSION TWO: Push press 8(5) (70%); Bench press 8(5)(70%); Bent over row 8(5) (70%); Deadlift 8(5)(70%); Cleans 8(4) (60%)
SESSION THREE: Row 200m (6) (RPE 10); **Run** 40s (10) (RPE 10)

Week 5

SESSION ONE: Bench press 5 (90%); MB press 10 (5); Lat Pulldown 5 (90%); MBl bounce 10 (5); Shoulder press 5 (90%); MB throw 10(5)
SESSION TWO: Skipping 1min (3); Tuck jumps 15; Squat jumps 15; Bounding 20m; Vertical jumps 15; Lateral obstacle jumps 15; (5)
SESSION THREE: Push press 8(5) (70%); Bench press 8(5)(70%); Bent over row 8(5) (70%); Deadlift 8(5)(70%); Cleans 8(4) (60%)

Week 6

SESSION ONE: Row 200m (8) (RPE 10); **Run** 40s (10) (RPE 10)
SESSION TWO: Clap press ups 15; MB trunk rotation 15; MB throw 15; MB bounce 15; DB punches (2-4kg) 30s; Burpees 20; (5)
SESSION THREE: Skipping 1min (3); Tuck jumps 15; Squat jumps 15; Bounding 20m; Vertical jumps 15; Lateral obstacle jumps 15; (6)

Week 7

SESSION ONE: Squats 6 (95%); Squat jumps 15; Lunges 6 (95%); Lunge jumps 10; Calf raises 20; Vertical jumps 10; (5); Falling starts and sprint 40m (10)
SESSION TWO: Push press 10(5) (70%); Bench press 10(5)(70%); Bent over row 10(5) (70%); Deadlift 8(5)(70%); Cleans 8(4) (70%)
SESSION THREE: Row Continuous 5mins (RPE 5); Interval (RPE 10:4) 10s:50s; 20s:40s; 30s:30s; 20s:40s; 10s:50s (3)

Week 8

SESSION ONE: Two-legged bounding 10; Tuck jumps 20; Burpees 20(3); Clap press ups; Med ball bounces 45s (3); Run 2min (10) (RPE 9)
SESSION TWO: Bench press 5 (100%); MB press 10 (5); Lat Pulldown 5 (100%); MBl bounce 10 (5); Shoulder press 5 (100%); MB throw 10(5)
SESSION THREE: Squats 6 (95%); Squat jumps 15; Lunges 6 (95%); Lunge jumps 10; Calf raises 20; Vertical jumps 10; (5); Falling starts and sprint 50m (8)

PROGRAMME 18:

Type of programme: Power training
Level: High fitness programme (perfect for vastly experienced exercisers looking to achieve significant performance improvements in their explosive power)

Week 1

SESSION ONE: Squat jumps; Lateral jumps; Power skipping; Vertical jumps; Burpees (80 of each in total throughout the session)
SESSION TWO: High knee jogging; Lunge into high knee; Side to side

ankle hops ; Standing jump and reach ; Front cone hops; Burpees with press ups 15 (3) Medium intensity;
SESSION THREE: Squats 8(5) (80%); Deadlift 8(5) (80%); Bench press 8(5) (80%); Bent over row 10(3) (70%); Shoulder press 10(3) (70%)

Week 2

SESSION ONE: MB trunk rotation 15; MB throw 15; MB bounce 15; DB punches (2-4kg) 45s; Burpees 20; (6)
SESSION TWO: Squats 6(6) (85%); Deadlift 6(6) (85%); Bench press 6(6) (85%); Bent over row 8(5) (80%); Shoulder press 8(5) (80%)
SESSION THREE: Cycle 500m (10) (RPE 9); **Row** 150m (8) (RPE 9)

Week 3

SESSION ONE: Squat jumps; Lateral jumps; Power skipping; Vertical jumps; Burpees (100 of each in total throughout the session)
SESSION TWO: Cycle and row Interval (RPE 10:4) 10s:50s; 20s:40s; 30s:30s; 20s:40s; 10s:50s (2 on each equipment) (RPE 10); **Run** 30s (10) (RPE 10)
SESSION THREE: Push press 10(4) (70%); Bench press 10(4)(70%); Bent over row 10(4) (70%); Deadlift 10(4)(70%); Cleans 8(3) (60%)

Week 4

SESSION ONE: Squats 6 (90%); Squat jumps 15; Lunges 6 (90%); Lunge jumps 10; Calf raises 20; Vertical jumps 10; (5); Falling starts and sprint 30m (10)
SESSION TWO: Push press 8(5) (70%); Bench press 8(5)(70%); Bent over row 8(5) (70%); Deadlift 8(5)(70%); Cleans 8(4) (60%)
SESSION THREE: Cycle and row Interval (RPE 10:4) 10s:50s; 20s:40s; 30s:30s; 40s:20s; 50s:10s (2 on each equipment) (RPE10); **Run** 30s (10) (RPE10)

Week 5

SESSION ONE: Bench press 5 (90%); MB press 10 (5); Lat Pulldown 5 (90%); MBl bounce 10 (5); Shoulder press 5 (90%); MB throw 10(5)
SESSION TWO: Skipping 1min (3); Tuck jumps 15; Squat jumps 15; Bounding 20m; Vertical jumps 15; Lateral obstacle jumps 15; (5)

SESSION THREE: Push press 8(5) (80%); Bench press 8(5)(80%); Bent over row 8(5) (80%); Deadlift 8(5)(80%); Cleans 8(4) (70%)

Week 6

SESSION ONE: Row 200m (10) (RPE 10); **Run** 40s (10) (RPE 10)
SESSION TWO: Clap press ups 15; MB trunk rotation 15; MB throw 15; MB bounce 15; DB punches (2-4kg) 30s; Burpees 20; (5)
SESSION THREE: Skipping 1min (5); Tuck jumps 20; Squat jumps 20; Bounding 30m; Vertical jumps 20; Lateral obstacle jumps 20; (6)

Week 7

SESSION ONE: Squats 6 (95%); Squat jumps 15; Lunges 6 (95%); Lunge jumps 10; Calf raises 20; Vertical jumps 10; (5); Falling starts and sprint 40m (10)
SESSION TWO: Push press 10(5) (80%); Bench press 10(5)(80%); Bent over row 10(5) (80%); Deadlift 8(5)(80%); Cleans 8(5) (70%)
SESSION THREE: Row Continuous 5mins (RPE 5); Interval (RPE 10:4) 10s:50s; 20s:40s; 30s:30s; 20s:40s; 10s:50s (5)

Week 8

SESSION ONE: Two-legged bounding 10; Tuck jumps 20; Burpees 20(3); Clap press ups; Med ball bounces 45s (3); Run 100m (10) (RPE 10)
SESSION TWO: Bench press 5 (100%); MB press 10 (5); Lat Pulldown 5 (100%); MBl bounce 10 (5); Shoulder press 5 (100%); MB throw 10(5)
SESSION THREE: Squats 6 (100%); Squat jumps 15; Lunges 6 (100%); Lunge jumps 10; Calf raises 20; Vertical jumps 10; (5); Falling starts and sprint 50m (8)

8

ULTIMATE CONDITIONING WORKOUTS

For those of you who are attempting a multi-disciplinary approach to training, I have put together two six-week ultimate conditioning workouts. These sessions will prepare you for any race or event that demands a mix of strength, power and endurance. Whilst training for multiple disciplines can sometimes be to the detriment of specific gains in the individual areas, these sessions will ensure that you are in tip top shape for whatever you have on the horizon.

YOUR CONDITIONING TRAINING PROGRAMMES

PROGRAMME 19

Type of programme: Ultimate conditioning workouts
Level: High fitness programme (perfect for experienced exercisers who have multiple fitness goals requiring a mixed programme)

Week 1

SESSION ONE: Cycle Continuous 5mins (RPE 5); Interval (RPE 10:4) 10s:50s; 20s:40s; 30s:30s; 20s:40s; 10s:50s (3); Squat jumps 20; Two-legged bounding 20m; Sprints 20m (5)
SESSION TWO: Supersets: Squats 6(5) (90%); Tuck jumps 10 (5); Bench press 6(5) (90%); Clap press ups 10(5); Bent over row 6(3) (90%); MB bounce 10 (3); Shoulder press 6(3) (90%); MB overhead wall throws 10(3)

SESSION THREE: Ascending pyramids: Bench Press; Lat Pulldown; Shoulder Press; Squats; Biceps curl; Triceps pushdown; 15(60%); 12(70%); 10(75%); 8(85%); 5(90%)

Week 2

SESSION ONE: Run 1km; 800m; 600m; 400m; 200m; 100m (Rest 180s; 150s; 120s; 90s; 60s; 180s) (2)
SESSION TWO: Tri sets: DB Shoulder press; Lat raise; Upright row; Chest flyes; Press ups; Decline bench press; Lat pulldown; Single arm row; Lower back extension 8(4) (85%); **Row** Intervals 100m:100m (10) (RPE 9:6)
SESSION THREE: Burpees; Ab crunches; Squats (85%); Pull ups; Triceps dips; Press ups (50 reps of each throughout the session)

Week 3

SESSION ONE: Squats 10(4) (90%); Deadlift 10(4) (90%); Bench press 10(4) (90%); Bent over row 10(4) (90%); Shoulder press 10(4) (90%); **Run** 1km (as quick as possible)
SESSION TWO: Row 1km; **Cycle** 8km; **Run** 1500m (2)
SESSION THREE: Squats 5 (90%); Squat jumps 10; Lunges 5 (90%); Lunge jumps 10; Calf raises 5 (85%); Vertical jumps 10; (6); Tuck jumps 20; Two-legged bounding 20m; (4); Sprints 20m (8)

Week 4

SESSION ONE: Lat Pulldown 8(5) (90%); Deadlift 8(5) (90%); Single arm row 8(5) (90%); Upright row 8(5) (90%); Shoulder press 8(5) (90%); Lat raise 8(5) (90%); Biceps curl 8(5) (90%); Hammer curl 8(5) (90%); Punch bag/Pad work 1min (3)
SESSION TWO: Run 2km; 1km; 500m; 200m; 100m (Rest 3mins; 90s; 45s; 20s; 3mins) (2)
SESSION THREE: Clap press ups 15; MB trunk rotation 15; MB throw 15; MB bounce 15; DB punches (2-4kg) 30s; Burpees 20; (5)

Week 5

SESSION ONE: Strip sets: Chest flyes; Lat raise; Bent arm pullover; Biceps curl; Triceps pushdown; Leg press; **Row** Intervals 200m:200m (3)

(RPE 9:6)
SESSION TWO: Burpees; Ab crunches; Squats (85%); Pull ups; Triceps dips; Press ups; Cleans (85%); Push press (70%) (40 reps of each throughout the session)
SESSION THREE: Run 40mins (RPE 7)

Week 6

SESSION ONE: Squats 8(4) (95%); Deadlift 8(4) (95%); Bench press 8(4) (95%); Bent over row 8(4) (95%); Shoulder press 8(4) (95%); **Run** 1km (as quick as possible)
SESSION TWO: Row 2km; **Cycle** 15km; **Run** 3km
SESSION THREE: Clap press ups 15; MB trunk rotation 15; MB throw 15; MB bounce 15; DB punches (2-4kg) 1min; Depth jumps 18" 10; Single leg bounding 15; (5)

PROGRAMME 20

Type of programme: Ultimate conditioning workouts
Level: High fitness programme (perfect for experienced exercisers who have multiple fitness goals requiring a mixed programme)

Week 1

SESSION ONE: Sprint starts from the floor 30m (10); Backward sprints 30m (10); Depth jumps18" 8 (5); Burpees with press ups 8(5); Push press 10(3) (75%) ; Bench press 10(3)(75%); Bent over row 10(3) (75%); Deadlift 10(3)(75%); Cleans 8 (3) (60%)
SESSION TWO: Row Intervals 1km (3) (RPE 8); **Cycle** Continuous 10km (RPE 7)
SESSION THREE: Run 40mins (RPE 7)

Week 2

SESSION ONE: Full pyramids: Bench Press; Lat Pulldown; Shoulder Press; Squats; Biceps curl; Triceps pushdown; 12(80%); 10(90%); 8(100%); 4(110%); 8(100%); 10(90%);12(80%)
SESSION TWO: Row 750m; **Cycle** 8km; **Run** 1500m (3)
SESSION THREE: Punches; Tuck jumps; Jackknifes; Burpees; Press ups; Shuttle runs; Weighted crunches 1min (6)

Week 3

SESSION ONE: Lat Pulldown 8(5) (90%); Deadlift 8(5) (90%); Single arm row 8(5) (90%); Upright row 8(5) (90%); Shoulder press 8(5) (90%); Lat raise 8(5) (90%); Biceps curl 8(5) (90%); Hammer curl 8(5) (90%);
SESSION TWO: Row Intervals 250m:100m (4) (RPE 10:3); **Cycle** Interval (RPE 10:4) 10s:50s; 20s:40s; 30s:30s; 40s: 20s; 50s: 10s (2)
SESSION THREE: Squats 8 (95%); Squat jumps 15; **Run** 1km (RPE 8) (4)

Week 4

SESSION ONE: Strip sets: Chest flyes; Lat raise; Bent arm pullover; Biceps curl; Triceps pushdown; Leg press; **Cycle** Intervals 500m:500m (3) (RPE 9:6)
SESSION TWO: Tuck jumps; Weighted crunches; Split jump lunges; Pull ups; Triceps dips; Clap press ups; Cleans (85%) Push press (50 reps of each throughout the session)
SESSION THREE: Run 45mins (RPE 7)

Week 5

SESSION ONE: Run 1km; 500m; 200m; 500m; 1km (Rest 2min; 1min; 30s; 1min; 2min) (2)
SESSION TWO: Full pyramids: Bench Press; Lat Pulldown; Shoulder Press; Squats; Biceps curl; Triceps pushdown; 12(80%); 10(90%); 8(100%); 4(110%); 8(100%); 10(90%);12(80%)
SESSION THREE: Row 1km; **Cycle** 10km; **Run** 2km (2)

Week 6

SESSION ONE: Clap press ups 20; MB trunk rotation 20; MB throw 20; MB bounce 20; DB punches (2-4kg) 45s; Burpees 20; (5)
SESSION TWO: Squats 10(5) (100%); Deadlift 10(5) (100%); Bench press 10(5) (100%); Bent over row 10(5) (100%); Shoulder press 10(5) (100%); **Row** Intervals 250m:100m (4) (RPE 9:3)
SESSION THREE: Row 2km; **Cycle** 15km; **Run** 3km

REFERENCES

Borg G., Linderholm H., 1967, Perceived exertion and pulse rate during graded exercise in various age groups, Acta Medica Scandinavica, 181, 194-206

Fox S. M., Naughton J. P., Haskell W. L., 1971, Physical activity and the prevention of coronary heart disease, Ann Clin Res, 3, 404-432

McArdle W. D., Katch F. I, Katch V. L., 2001, Exercise Physiology: Energy, Nutrition and Human Performance (Fifth edition). Lippincott Williams & Wilkins, Philadelphia, PA

ALSO OUT NOW

If you enjoyed this book you may also be interested in reading:

The need to know guide to nutrition and exercise
By Tim Shaw BSc MSC

Available now on Amazon.com

www.ymcaed.org.uk/gne

Central YMCA Guides
Trustworthy advice from those in the know

Discover more books and ebooks of interest to you and find out about the range of work we do at the forefront of health, fitness and wellbeing.

www.ymcaed.org.uk

Date Completed: 11/02/2015

Printed in Great Britain
by Amazon.co.uk, Ltd.,
Marston Gate.